Confidently
YOU

Confidently
YOU

JOYCE MEYER

New York • Nashville

FaithWords
Hachette Book Group
1290 Avenue of the Americas, New York, NY 10104
faithwords.com
twitter.com/faithwords

First Edition: July 2022

FaithWords is a division of Hachette Book Group, Inc. The FaithWords name and logo are trademarks of Hachette Book Group, Inc.

The publisher is not responsible for websites (or their content) that are not owned by the publisher.

The Hachette Speakers Bureau provides a wide range of authors for speaking events. To find out more, go to www.hachettespeakersbureau.com or call (866) 376-6591.

Scripture notations located on page 108.

Print book interior design by Bart Dawson

Library of Congress Cataloging-in-Publication Data

Names: Meyer, Joyce, 1943- author.
Title: Confidently you / Joyce Meyer.
Description: First edition. | Nashville : FaithWords, [2022] | Includes
  bibliographical references.
Identifiers: LCCN 2021053873 | ISBN 9781546013518 (hardcover) |
  ISBN 9781546015482 (ebook)
Subjects: LCSH: Christian women—Religious life. | Self-confidence—Religious
  aspects--Christianity.
Classification: LCC BV4527 .M43822 2022 | DDC 248.8/43—dc23/
  eng/20220113
LC record available at https://lccn.loc.gov/2021053873

ISBNs: 978-1-5460-1351-8 (paper over board), 978-1-5460-1548-2 (ebook)

Printed in the United States of America

LSC-C

Printing 1, 2022

CONTENTS

INTRODUCTION

When you see a confident person, you recognize their confidence right away. You notice it in the way they walk and hold their head up high. You hear it in the way they talk. You perceive it in the way they deal with other people. And you see it in the successes they enjoy.

I believe confidence is the key to much success and fulfillment in life, and I am glad you have chosen to take the journey toward becoming confidently you. Whether you view yourself as someone who is fairly confident most of the time, someone who has almost no confidence at all, or someone in between, I believe the lessons in these pages will give you a greater understanding of what true confidence is and how it operates and manifests in the life of a godly person.

Confidence is a quality that most people admire and want but sometimes struggle to develop. The good news is that confidence is a quality anyone can have. It's not like height, eye color, a beautiful singing voice, or other characteristics people are born with. Confidence is like discipline or physical strength; it can be developed. If you think, *I am just not a confident person*, that can change. You can be confident—starting today.

Though confidence is often associated with people who have strong personalities, you can also be quiet and reserved, studious and serious, or relaxed and laid back, yet confident at the same time. Becoming confident doesn't mean you take on a different personality. It means you become the best, most courageous, most positive version of yourself.

As you grow in confidence, you will be amazed by the possibilities that open up for you and the ways you can flourish and enjoy your life. The first step toward a confident you is to change the way you think about yourself and about God. Once you realize how God thinks about you and learn to see yourself as He sees you, confidence follows. A good prayer to pray before you go further in this book would be: "Lord, help me to grow in confidence as I come to understand how You think about me. I choose today to agree with the way You see me and, based on that, to become my most confident self."

Confidence has become a buzzword in secular society—what the Bible calls "the world." Usually, when people think of confidence, they think of self-confidence. The world applauds this kind of confidence and urges everyone to develop it to the greatest possible degree.

The world often considers people with low confidence deficient in a quality necessary for success and views confidence as the solution for all kinds of problems. For example, our society says that if people aren't performing well at work or if their social life is boring, they simply need to be more confident. There are so many resources to help people be confident that it almost boggles the mind. Just think about how many times you hear television self-help gurus, celebrities, or athletes urging you to believe in yourself! I'm sure that if we knew how much money people spend in the United States each year trying to boost their self-confidence, we would be shocked.

I wish the world knew that self-confidence isn't as valuable as many people think. It may help people accomplish certain goals, but it requires them to rely on their own strength and effort. There's a lot of striving involved in developing self-confidence, and striving can leave people feeling exhausted and frustrated. Reaching goals through the power of self-confidence isn't always fulfilling, so people then set new goals and drain their strength to achieve them. Ultimately, confidence that is entirely self-focused and self-energized doesn't lead to much satisfaction.

I have walked the journey from self-confidence to confidence in God, and I want to make clear from the start of this book that our confidence must be in Christ alone, not in our human strength or abilities, not in other people, and not in the world or its systems.

Worldly confidence won't take you where you truly

need to go in life, but confidence in God will enable you
to live a life beyond anything you have ever imagined.
Self-confidence may help you work *your* plan for your
life, but confidence in God will empower you to live in
His plan, which is far better than anything you could want
for yourself. To be confident in Christ means that you
trust Him to enable you to do whatever you need to do.

At the end of each chapter of this book, you will see questions designed to help you grow in confidence and scriptures that I refer to as "Confidence Boosters" because as
you study them, they will strengthen you to become your
most confident self.

I am praying for you to become more confidently
you, and I believe that your growing confidence in God
will bring an abundance of His blessings, strength, fulfillment, and joy into your life.

CHAPTER 1

Where Does Your Confidence Come From?

Confidence in the natural world is self-reliance;
in the spiritual world it is God-reliance.

Oswald Chambers

When you think of a confident person, what image comes to mind? Do you envision someone with a strong personality—someone who knows how to work a room, easily striking up a conversation with anyone and everyone? Do you think of someone who sits down at a business meeting knowing exactly what they want and how they will get it, then executes their plan successfully? Do you think of a singer or a public speaker who feels more comfortable performing in front of a large audience than sitting with a friend in a coffee shop? Maybe you think of an athlete who is enormously talented and knows it—and has a swagger that intimidates opponents. Or perhaps you think of that person in your group of friends who joins a few of you for lunch and quickly dominates the conversation.

We all have our impressions of what confidence looks like in other people. The important question is, what does confidence look like in *you*? I didn't write this book so you could become confidently someone else, but so you can become confidently you.

TWO TYPES OF CONFIDENCE

To be confident is to live boldly and without fear and to believe you will succeed. You can try to find confidence in yourself, or you can definitely find it in God. Before we go too far in your journey toward becoming your most confident self, let me say that there are two kinds of confidence. The type of confidence you will have depends on its source. One kind is the confidence people find in themselves that is rooted in their human strength, the force of their personality, and their natural abilities. Philippians 3:3 refers to this as "confidence in the flesh," but we usually call it "self-confidence," thinking this quality depends on a person's natural inner resources. People who are filled with self-confidence are quick to tell others about their own strong points and good qualities, believing they have produced those positive attributes in themselves. Instead of being grateful to God for their strengths, they take credit for them.

The other type of confidence is also personal in

nature, but it's rooted in dependence on God, not self. It comes from knowing God's love and acceptance, and from the humble realization that apart from Him, we can do nothing (John 15:5). I call this godly confidence or confidence in God because it draws its strength from the never-ending resources God offers us. People with this type of confidence are quick to recognize that the good things about them come from God, and they are thankful for the ways He has blessed them.

The apostle Paul understood the difference between self-confidence and godly confidence. In Philippians 3, he mentions the reasons he could have found confidence in himself. He actually says in Philippians 3:4: "If someone else thinks they have reasons to put confidence in the flesh, I have more." Then he lists some of his impressive credentials and accomplishments (vv. 5–6), but in the next chapter, he explains that he does all things in Christ's strength, not in his own:

> I can do all things [which He has called me to do] through Him who strengthens and empowers me [to fulfill His purpose—I am self-sufficient in Christ's sufficiency; I am ready for anything and equal to anything through Him who infuses me with inner strength and confident peace.]
>
> Philippians 4:13 AMP

Based on this verse, we might also say that we can all be confident through Christ's confidence, meaning the confidence He gives us because we are in Him. Another way I like to say this is that we have confidence only because Christ lives in us, and it is His confidence that we draw on. I do want you to have confidence in yourself, but only if that confidence is rooted in God.

I challenge you to believe (have faith) that you can be confident with the confidence that comes from God. Even if you have never felt confident about anything in your life, even if you have never been especially courageous or bold, or even if you have a laid-back personality that people don't associate with confidence, you *can* be confident. It is a decision you make, while leaning entirely on Jesus, and a sense of strength and boldness you have *within* yourself, but it does not come from anything you are, anything you have, or anything you can do as a result of mere human strength. I often tell people that they can *be* confident even if they don't *feel* confident because it is based on faith, not feelings.

There are times when I step out on the stage at one of our conferences and don't particularly feel confident. But when I continue stepping toward the podium in faith, God always gives me the confidence (grace) to do what I need to do.

THE BEST KIND OF CONFIDENCE

When developing self-confidence, people place their trust in all kinds of things—their job, their spouse, their savings account, their knowledge or education, or their talents and abilities. The problem with putting confidence in any of these things is that they are all subject to change, sometimes significantly and quickly. And if something can change, it is really not a good place to place your confidence.

I am convinced that the only place worthy of our confidence is in God. Unlike everything and everyone else, He is unshakable. He never changes. He is "the same yesterday and today and forever" (Hebrews 13:8). Confidence in God is different from any other kind of confidence, and it is the deepest, strongest, longest-lasting, best kind of confidence you can have.

What exactly is confidence in God? It is absolute trust in who God is—His character and His nature—and it is the confidence that comes from being in personal relationship with Him. It is the deeply held conviction that He is trustworthy, that He will always make good on His promises, and that He has a wonderful plan for your life and wants to help you fulfill it. To be confident in Him means that you know beyond a shadow of a doubt that you can do anything you need to do in life through Christ who strengthens you (Philippians 4:13) and that God works every situation in your life for your good because you love Him and are called according to His purpose (Romans 8:28). Confidence in God brings deep fulfillment and demands no striving at all. All you have to do is believe what His Word says about you and rest in those truths. Confidence in God doesn't call for self-effort; it depends on His grace.

YOU NEVER HAVE TO LOSE CONFIDENCE IN GOD

You may remember the story of Nehemiah. This Jewish man, in exile in Persia, worked in the king's court and heard that the wall of Jerusalem had been broken down when the Babylonians destroyed the city and took the Jewish people into exile. He was so grieved about this that he asked the king's permission to go to Jerusalem and lead the effort to rebuild the wall. The king agreed.

Nehemiah and his helpers faced all kinds of opposition as they tried to reconstruct the wall, but they eventually finished it. When their enemies heard about this, according to Nehemiah 6:16, "all the surrounding nations were afraid and lost their self-confidence, because they realized that this work had been done with the help of our God."

You can see from this story that it is possible, maybe even easy, to lose your self-confidence. All it takes is a little fear or intimidation, or perhaps a mistake or a disappointment, and self-confidence can vanish. This is because human strength is fickle. Sometimes you feel strong and sometimes you feel weak. But God never changes (Hebrews 13:8). He is always strong. Therefore, He will never fail you or be weak; you can trust Him at all times.

When you have confidence in God, you know that He is always there to help you, and you can live in freedom and boldness. You are open to learning new things and taking risks, because you know your confidence allows you to embrace life's opportunities boldly, eager to discover what awaits you. You know that every unknown is a chance to learn more about yourself, grow in God, and move toward fulfilling all the potential He has placed within you.

QUESTIONS TO HELP YOU
GROW IN CONFIDENCE

1. What is the difference between self-confidence and godly confidence?

2. In what specific area of your life do you need to grow in godly confidence? Ask God to help you develop that kind of trust and confidence as you read this book.

CONFIDENCE BOOSTERS

For we who worship by the Spirit of God…rely on what Christ Jesus has done for us. We put no confidence in human effort.

Philippians 3:3 NLT

We should not trust in ourselves but in God.

2 Corinthians 1:9 NKJV

I am convinced and confident of this very thing, that He who has begun a good work in you will [continue to] perfect and complete it until the day of Christ Jesus.

Philippians 1:6 AMP

CHAPTER 2

The Blessings of Confidence in God

*It is when our self-confidence is finally
destroyed and is replaced with dependence
upon God that we have victory.*

K. P. Yohannan, *When We Have Failed—What Next?*

Finding your confidence in God will bring many blessings to your life. It will remind you that you are loved unconditionally. It will empower you to accept yourself, setting you free from people-pleasing and pretending to be someone you are not. (I will write about this later in the book.) It will strengthen you against all kinds of fear—especially fear of the future, rejection, making mistakes, and disappointment. Being confident in God will also give you courage to take risks when He calls you do something by faith. It will provide you with the assurance that He is always trustworthy, in control, and working for your good when you do not understand why certain things have happened or not happened for you.

In this chapter, I want to focus on three specific benefits you can expect from placing your confidence in God. First, confidence in God brings out the best in you. It enables you to be your strongest, happiest, most productive, and most fulfilled self. Second, it gives you the sense of security you need to boldly discover and pursue His purpose for your life. Third, confidence in God guarantees His victory in every battle you face.

CONFIDENCE IN GOD BRINGS OUT THE BEST IN YOU

Imagine you're a member of a basketball team, and your captain is the most talented, most court-savvy player in the world. Not only can this athlete outplay anyone else on the court, but they also bring out the best in their teammates. You can enter each game with confidence, knowing that your team captain has the knowledge and skill to lead you to victory. Sure, you will need to do your part and fulfill your role on the team, but even if you have an off game, your superstar will have you covered. They have your back. And as each game unfolds, you find that your leader's confidence is contagious. You can play boldly, because your captain inspires you.

I think of myself as a confident person, and I hope you will view yourself as confident too as a result of reading this book. When I say I am confident, I don't mean I am confident in myself or in my abilities. I mean that

I am confident in my leader, God, and in the gifts, talents, and knowledge He has placed in me. I know that without Him, I "can do nothing" (John 15:5), but that with Him, I can be a champion, because He brings out the best in me. There have been times when I have made the mistake of being self-confident. When that happens, I always fail, and I am glad that I do, because I want Jesus to always remind me that apart from Him I can do nothing (John 15:5).

Many people never experience the best that is in them or the best that God has for them because they live in fear instead of confidence. You may have missed out on some good things in life because fear held you captive. You may be living with certain regrets because you were not confident enough to do some things that could have made a difference in your life. If so, let me encourage you in two ways: First, let me simply say that God loves you, and He wants you to relax in the knowledge of His love. He wants you to experience the peace of mind that comes from resting in His love and living without the torment of fear and doubt. Second, let me also say that God is a redeemer and a restorer. In Him, there are no lost opportunities. He has a way of bringing things back around. They may not be exactly the same opportunities you passed up previously, but they may be better. If God wants you to accomplish or experience something, He will give you another chance.

CONFIDENCE IN GOD
BRINGS SECURITY

A confident person feels safe. They believe they are loved, valuable, cared for, and safe in God's will. They feel free, as I mentioned earlier, to explore and pursue His purpose and plan for their life. When you feel safe and secure, knowing that God is guiding you and watching over you, stepping out and trying new things is easy and even exciting.

When people feel safe, they are at liberty to take risks in order to try to succeed. When we know we are loved for ourselves and not just for our accomplishments or performance, we no longer need to fear failure. We realize that failing at something does not make us a failure at everything.

When we feel secure in God, we are free to explore, live an adventurous life, and find out what we are best suited for. We are free to find our own niche in life, which is not possible without stepping out. Trial and error pave the road to success, and you can't drive that road when your car is parked. So get moving, and God will direct you. When people are confident, they try things, and they keep trying until they find a way to be successful in what God has called them to do.

At various points in our lives, all of us feel we're in over our heads or out of our depth. The reality is that without God, we're always in over our heads. We may face problems such as the loss of a job, the death of a loved one, strife in our family, financial difficulties, or a bad report from the doctor. When these things happen, we are tempted to panic because we feel we've lost control. But the truth is that we never have been in control in the first place. We've always been held by the grace of God, our Father, and that won't change. God is never out of His depth, and we are always safe with Him.

CONFIDENCE IN GOD ASSURES
HIS VICTORY IN YOUR LIFE

In 2 Chronicles 32:1, we read that the king of Assyria—an enemy of God's people in the land of Judah—invaded Judah and tried to take over the cities. Hezekiah, the king of Judah, encouraged his military leaders with these words: "With him is only the arm of flesh, but *with us is the Lord our God* to help us and to fight our battles" (2 Chronicles 32:8, emphasis mine).

Hezekiah's observation reminds us that there are two types of confidence—self-confidence, which he calls "the arm of flesh," and confidence that comes from knowing God. He was reminding his leaders that the arm of flesh is no match for the presence of God. Because God was with the people of Judah, Hezekiah knew that He would help them and give them victory.

If you are a believer, God is with you, just as He was with the people of Judah. He is always there to help you and to fight your battles. You never have to do anything alone, and you are never helpless. God has more power and strength than any force on earth, and if He is with you, you can relax and let Him fight on your behalf, knowing He will always give you victory and He will never let you down. Now *that* is a reason to be confident.

Confidence in God allows you to face life with boldness, openness, and honesty. It enables you to live without worry and to feel safe, knowing you can trust Him in every situation. And it ensures His victory in your life, no matter what battles you face. When you put your confidence in anything or anyone other than God, you risk being disappointed. But when you place your confidence in Christ, who is all-loving, all-wise, and all-powerful, He will never fail you.

As you grow in confidence in God, you will find many blessings, far more than the ones I have described in this chapter. You may be blessed in ways you have never known before and in ways I haven't mentioned. God loves you and wants to bless you, and there is no limit to the ways He can do that.

QUESTIONS TO HELP YOU
GROW IN CONFIDENCE

1. When you think about the realities of your life, in what ways could you benefit most from having confidence in God?

2. What could keep you from experiencing the blessings of a life that is confident in God? How can you change that?

CONFIDENCE BOOSTERS

Blessed is the one who trusts in the Lord, whose confidence is in him.

Jeremiah 17:7

In him and through faith in him we may approach God with freedom and confidence.

Ephesians 3:12

And God is able to bless you abundantly, so that in all things at all times, having all that you need, you will abound in every good work.

2 Corinthians 9:8

CHAPTER 3

Who, Me? Bold?

As disciples, we find not some
but all of our strength, hope, courage,
and confidence in God.

Henri Nouwen, Donald P. McNeill,
and Douglas A. Morrison, *Compassion*

Maybe you've stayed with me this far and you're still thinking, *Joyce, I am a shy, timid person—that's just my nature. I wouldn't even feel like myself if I acted confident and bold. I just don't think I can change!* You may feel timid and shy, but you can choose to walk boldly through life. Your feelings don't have to determine your attitude, and it's time for a confident, courageous attitude. This doesn't mean becoming loud or aggressive. You can keep your sweet, reserved personality and still have a bold disposition on the inside.

The main truth I want you to remember is that you can feel afraid, timid, or downright cowardly and still *decide* to walk boldly—as though the fear does not exist. Fear can be present in all kinds of situations, but when you choose to ignore it, it has no power over you. As I have said often, "You can do it afraid."

Your free will (God-given ability to make choices) is stronger than your feelings if you will exercise it. Many people have catered to their feelings for so long that their emotions now control them. Perhaps you have allowed this to happen to you. If so, the good news is that your will is like a muscle; it becomes weak if not exercised, but the more you use it, the stronger it grows. As you begin to ask God to help you and exercise your willpower against your feelings, choosing to be brave instead of fearful, becoming the person you truly want to be—the one God designed and intends for you to be—will get easier and easier.

A WORD OF CAUTION

Some people are naturally outgoing or outspoken and may be considered bold, type A, or extroverted. People may refer to them as having a strong personality. These people have to overcome pride, bossiness, aggression, and false confidence. Like everyone, a type-A person has strong points and also has tendencies that need to be worked on and overcome. Believe me, I know what I am talking about because I am that type-A personality who loves to give direction and be in control. God has dealt very strongly with me about the foolishness of self-confidence and the wisdom of having my confidence in Him alone. The Book of Proverbs often refers to the fool as "the self-confident fool."

The opposite of a type-A person is the introvert, or someone who is shy, timid, and reserved. This kind of person needs to overcome shyness, timidity, fear, the temptation to withdraw from challenges, and low confidence. I mention this because although this chapter focuses on boldness and I am clear about some areas in which a naturally bold person may need to improve, I don't want to single out the extroverts. I want to point out that every personality type has areas that need improvement. That's the way God made us.

A bold person can often be assertive to the point of being rude. Sometimes, what people think is boldness is, in reality, pride, which is something God's Word says that He hates (Proverbs 6:16–17). I am a naturally bold person, and I have had to stand against pride. It seems that bold people simply assume they are right about most things, and they don't mind telling other people just how right they are. While confidence is a good quality, this kind of egotism is not true godly confidence. Thank God we can learn to have balance in our lives. We can benefit from our strengths and overcome our weaknesses with His help. But we must lean on Him continually or we will backslide into old bad habits.

TRUE BOLDNESS DOESN'T IGNORE FEAR

Some people think they are bold, but they are merely rude, aggressive, and impudent. They would be much better off being honest and admitting that they are not as confident as they appear, but many of them struggle to do that. I must admit that I pretended to be brave for many years, even though I was filled with various kinds of fear. I thought I was a bold woman, but the truth is that underneath the pretense, I was very fearful and insecure. I tried to convince myself—and everyone around me—that I was not afraid of anything, which kept me from confronting my fears and dealing with them in a healthy way.

There is a difference between truly facing fear and simply ignoring it. When people pretend they are not afraid but they really are, they are not able to genuinely overcome their fears and develop true courage. They simply try to cover their fears with phony boldness. When they do this, they deceive themselves and are off-putting to others. If they would simply be honest about the fact that they are afraid in certain ways, they could receive help and strength from God and others. People will always be better off humbly telling the truth and saying, "I feel fear, but I will move forward anyway."

HOW TRUE BOLDNESS
HANDLES OFFENSE

Before I learned how to walk in true boldness, I was quick to speak my mind, but what I said was often foolish and inappropriate. I often took control of situations, thinking I would step out in boldness and do something since nobody else seemed to be doing anything, only to later realize that I had taken authority I should not have taken.

I frequently moved impatiently and too quickly, once again thinking I was bold, but I made many mistakes and hurt a lot of people because I did not take time to seek wisdom. I was really very immature and knew nothing about the kind of boldness and strength God can give.

If anyone offended or insulted me, I was quick to defend myself, put them in their place, and make clear that I would not be mistreated. However, as I became a student of God's Word in an effort to grow spiritually by His grace, I learned, matured, and received correction and instruction from scriptures such as these:

Fools show their annoyance at once, but the prudent overlook an insult.

Proverbs 12:16

Do not take revenge, my dear friends, but leave room
for God's wrath, for it is written: "It is mine to avenge;
I will repay," says the Lord.

Romans 12:19

Before I allowed God's Word to begin to change me,
I was quick to let people know when they offended me
and quick to try to vindicate myself. I thought I was bold,
not realizing that genuinely bold, courageous people not
only have the courage to take action but also demonstrate
patience and wisdom, and they always trust that God will
bring vengeance as needed in His timing and His way.

WHAT TRUE BOLDNESS LOOKS LIKE

A person who is genuinely bold and courageous is also
humble. Some people think boldness and humility are
mutually exclusive, but they are not. In fact, it's impossi-
ble to be truly bold without also being genuinely humble.
Authentic confidence embodies both qualities.

Think about various people in the Bible who did great
exploits, yet demonstrated great humility. For example:

- Moses led God's people out of Egypt, yet he
  reached a point when his leadership had become too much for him, so his father-in-law

recommended delegating certain tasks to others (Exodus 18:13–26).

- Mary, the mother of Jesus, was given the greatest honor on earth—to bring God's Son into the world. When the angel Gabriel announced God's plan to her, she acknowledged that the Lord had "been mindful of the humble state of his servant" (Luke 1:48).

- The apostle Paul traveled extensively, zealously spreading the gospel, and he wrote books of the Bible that we still live by today, yet he called himself the worst of sinners (1 Timothy 1:15).

These people and others throughout the Bible viewed themselves through the lens of humility. They knew their flaws, but they did not let their shortcomings cause them to back away from God's plan for their lives. They were humble enough to realize that they were nothing apart from Him, yet bold enough to say yes when He wanted to use them.

I pray that you will develop true boldness and confidence in your life and that you will walk in humility while also boldly following God, no matter what He calls you to do. Remember that true boldness demonstrates *courage in the face of fear*—not the *absence of fear*. Boldness requires wisdom, patience, and faith—not in your human strength, but in all that God can do through you.

QUESTIONS TO HELP YOU GROW IN CONFIDENCE

1. Why is facing fear so much better than ignoring it while pretending to be brave?

2. How has your perspective of boldness changed after reading this chapter? Ask God to give you a confident but humble heart.

CONFIDENCE BOOSTERS

When I called, you answered me; you greatly emboldened me.

Psalm 138:3

Though an army besiege me, my heart will not fear; though war break out against me, even then I will be confident.

Psalm 27:3

After they prayed…they were all filled with the Holy Spirit and spoke the word of God boldly.

Acts 4:31

CHAPTER 4

Live Loved

*Grace teaches us that God loves because of
who God is, not because of who we are.*
Philip Yancey, *What's So Amazing about Grace?*

Have you ever wondered why some people are confident and others are not? Maybe they were raised in the same family and share many of the same experiences. Perhaps they read the same books and attend the same social events. Maybe they attend the same church and they hear the same Bible teaching each week. They may sing together in worship, or sit together in a prayer group. Even though they have similar experiences, some are strong and confident while others are not. There may be several reasons for this, one of which is this: Some people have received and embraced God's love for them—the love He reveals to them directly and extends to them through other people—while others still struggle to do so.

People who know they are loved are much more confident than those who don't. It helps to believe they have the love of God and the love of the important people in their lives, but even when they aren't surrounded by huge amounts of human love, God's love is enough. People who are convinced that God loves them possess an inner strength and a confidence that nothing else can give—and nothing can take away. Consider Paul's words about the power of God's love:

> For I am convinced that neither death nor life, neither angels nor demons, neither the present nor the future, nor any powers, neither height nor depth, nor anything else in all creation, will be able to separate us from the love of God that is in Christ Jesus our Lord.
>
> Romans 8:38–39, emphasis mine

GOD LOVES YOU

There is no limit to how confident you can become when you know first and foremost that God loves you unconditionally. When this truth is settled in your heart, you will never again fear being rejected or unloved. You will rest in the fact that God loves and accepts you unconditionally, no matter what you do or how you may fail. God doesn't love it when we sin, but He *never* stops loving us. When you are not afraid of being unloved, you can live with remarkable boldness. Knowing you are loved will make you whole, complete, and strong on the inside.

Everyone desires and needs love and acceptance from God and from other people. Although not everyone will accept and love us, some will. We are wise to concentrate on those who do love us and not worry about those who don't. God certainly does love us, and He can provide others who love us too if we ask Him to lead us to the people He wants in our lives and show us whom to bring into our circle of inclusion.

We can sense and know God's love as He reveals it to us in our hearts, but we also experience it through the people He gives us to walk with on our journey through life. I believe we need what I call divine connections, meaning relationships that God orchestrates and brings into our lives. These are people through whom He can show us His love, people who will pray for us and ask Him to help us, and people who will encourage us with His Word.

I encourage you to pray about your circle of friends. Don't just decide that you want to be part of a certain social group and then try to get into it. Instead, follow the leading of the Holy Spirit in choosing those with whom you want to associate closely. He will help you recognize the people who will bless your life and whom you can bless in return, as you allow Him to guide you in relationships. God can give you favor with the people who are right for you—those who will add to your life and help you develop godly character.

If you recognize the need for love in your life, the place to start is with God. He is a Father who wants to shower love and blessings upon His children. If your natural father did not love you properly, you can receive from God what you missed in your childhood. Love is the healing balm that the world needs, and God offers it freely and continuously. His love is unconditional. He does not love us *if*…He simply and for all times loves us. He loves us because He is kind and because He desires to show us His love:

> For he chose us in him before the creation of the world to be holy and blameless in his sight. In love he predestined us for adoption to sonship through Jesus Christ, in accordance with his pleasure and will.
>
> Ephesians 1:4–5

Receiving the gift of God's unconditional love is the beginning of our healing, the foundation for our new life in Christ, and the cornerstone of our confidence. We cannot love ourselves unless we realize how much God loves us, and if we don't love ourselves, we cannot love other people. We cannot maintain good, healthy relationships without this foundation of love in our lives.

DESPERATE FOR LOVE

I grew up in an abusive, dysfunctional atmosphere and was filled with shame, blame, guilt, and disgrace by the time I was eighteen. This left me desperate for love, so I married very young simply because I was afraid no one would ever want me. The young man had problems of his own and did not really know how to love me—so the pattern of pain in my life continued, and the relationship ended in divorce after five years.

By the time I met my husband, Dave, to whom I have been married since 1967, I was desperate for love but did not know how to receive it even when it was available. Dave truly did love me, but I found myself constantly deflecting his love because of the way I felt about myself deep inside. As I entered into a serious and committed relationship with God through Jesus Christ, I began to learn about God's love, but fully accepting His love took a long time.

When you feel unlovable, getting the truth that God loves you perfectly even though you are not perfect through your head and into your heart can be difficult. No one on this earth will ever be perfect, but thankfully, God is not looking for perfection. He wants you to love Him and want His will, and He wants you to confess your sin and repent. God sees your heart, not just your behavior, and He realizes that there is a big difference between wickedness and weakness.

The apostle Peter, for example, had many weaknesses, but God still used him in a powerful way because he was not wicked. He loved Jesus greatly and was sorry for his sins. God loves and accepts you just the way you are, and He will help you get to where you need to be. You can read about this throughout the Bible. If you are not familiar with what the Bible says about God's love for you, I would suggest you start with Ephesians 1 and the short book of 1 John.

RECEIVE THE GIFT OF GOD'S LOVE

God's love is a gift that you cannot earn and cannot buy. He offers it freely and without condition. What do you do with a gift? Simply receive it and be grateful.

I urge you to take a step of faith right now and say aloud, "God loves me unconditionally, and I receive His love!" You may have to say it a hundred times a day, as I did for months, before it finally sinks in, but when it does, it will be the happiest day of your life. There is power in your words (Proverbs 18:21), and the more you remind yourself that God loves you, the more you will believe it.

To know that you are loved by someone you can trust is the best and most comforting feeling in the world. God will not only love you that way, but He will also provide other people who will truly love you. When He does bring them into your life, be sure to remain thankful for them. Having people who genuinely love you is a precious gift.

First John 4:18 says that God's perfect love "casts out fear" (NKJV). When we know we are loved by God, fear does not rule us, and that sets us free to be bold and confident.

QUESTIONS TO HELP YOU
GROW IN CONFIDENCE

1. What are two ways you can experience God's love? How is He showing you His love right now? How is He showing it to you through other people? For example, today I went shopping with my daughter, and she paid for my purchases as a blessing to me. I saw her actions as God loving me through her.

2. What is the key to being able to love yourself?

CONFIDENCE BOOSTERS

The steadfast love of the Lord never ceases; his mercies never come to an end; they are new every morning; great is your faithfulness.

Lamentations 3:22–23 ESV

I have loved you with an everlasting love; I have drawn you with unfailing kindness.

Jeremiah 31:3

We know and rely on the love God has for us. God is love. Whoever lives in love lives in God, and God in them.

1 John 4:16

CHAPTER 5

No Comparison

*Enjoy your own life without comparing it
with that of another.*

Nicolas de Condorcet, *Condorcet: Political Writings*

An important key to becoming confidently you is
understanding and embracing your uniqueness and
accepting yourself. You accept your strengths and weaknesses, your success and your mistakes, your good points
and your not-so-good points. You do not allow yourself
to fall into self-rejection or self-hatred, but you embrace
every unique quality that makes you who you are. This
does not mean you never try to improve in appropriate
ways, because God has given us the Holy Spirit to lead us
into all truth and to help us become more like Jesus, but
you do not need to compare yourself to others and then
try to be like they are or compete with them in an effort to
be the very best in every area of life.

I do not believe it is possible for anyone to be confident as long as they compare themself to others. Comparison is a waste of time and energy, which would be better
invested in making the most of who God created you to

be and enjoying that. He does not compare you with other people; He knows everything about you and loves you unconditionally, accepting you the way you are, so why should you compare yourself with anyone around you? Your weaknesses are not a surprise to God. He knew all about each one of them long before you discovered them, and He still chose you to be His special child.

While comparison does not serve people well, many people still struggle with it. If you are one of them, I believe this chapter will help you break free from the frustration of comparing yourself with someone else and enable you to live with boldness and confidence, enjoying the person God made you to be. You can enjoy your talents, abilities, and personality without comparing yourself to anyone else. Your uniqueness is what makes you special.

RESIST THE WORLD'S WAY

We live in a world that pushes us to compare ourselves with others and compete with them in terms of how we look, what we accomplish, how much we own, where we live, and even how "successful" our spouses or children are. In our society, certain things are considered better than others, and each day we see images or advertisements that push us to be or have the "best." God wants us to be our best for His glory, but we don't need to be like someone else in order to do that.

Sadly, some people spend time, energy, and money

they do not have pursuing what the world says they should have or achieve. Then, once they achieve it, it has been replaced with something people view as more desirable. I remember when people were happy to have any kind of phone in their car, but now even mobile phones have a hierarchy. Companies offer new models often, and people feel the need to upgrade, even if the phone they have works well and meets their needs.

Much advertising is geared to prod people to think they are somehow less than others if they do not look better or have more than those around them. We are bombarded with messages: If you wear *this* brand of clothes, people will know you are successful! If you use *this* face cream, you will look much younger than you really are! If you try *this* new diet and lose those few extra pounds, you will be more attractive and accepted! The world consistently gives us the impression that we need to be something other than what we are and that some product, program, or prescription can help us do it. There is nothing wrong with wanting to look our best or have nice things, but our motive for doing so should not be to keep up with someone else or look better than they do.

The fact is, no matter how good we look, how talented or smart we are, or how much success we achieve, somebody somewhere will look better, be smarter, or achieve more—and then we have to decide whether we want to compare and compete all over again. Always struggling to maintain the number one position is hard work. In fact, it's exhausting.

One of the Ten Commandments is "You shall not covet" (Exodus 20:17). This means we are not to lust after what other people have, how they look, their talents, their personality, or anything else about them. I believe lust is present when we want something so much that we cannot be happy without it.

Coveting what other people have is not pleasing to God. Another person can be an example to us, but should never be our standard. Paul writes in Philippians 4:11, "I have learned to be content whatever the circumstances." We would be wise to learn this lesson too. Whoever you are, whatever you can (or cannot) do, and whatever you have (or don't have), decide that you will be content with it and make the most of it. God knows exactly what you need and when you need it, and He will make sure that all your needs are met. His job is to meet your needs; yours is to be content with and grateful for all that He gives you, not comparing anything about your life with someone else's.

Romans 8:29 says that we are destined to be molded into the image of Jesus Christ and share inwardly His likeness. Another scripture says that we have the mind of Christ (1 Corinthians 2:16). This means that we can think, speak, and learn to behave as Jesus did, and He certainly did not ever compare Himself with anyone or desire to be anything other than what His Father had made Him to be. He lived to do the Father's will, not to compare Himself to others and compete with them. He found His disciples arguing over which of them was the greatest, and He said the greatest among you is the one who serves (Matthew 20:26–27). Only a confident person can serve others and do so with joy.

I believe confidence is found in doing the best we can with what we have to work with and not in comparing or competing with other people. In fact, when we have confidence, we never feel the need to compare or compete with anyone. We are never truly free until we no longer have a need to impress anyone. Real fulfillment and satisfaction come not from comparing ourselves to others, but in being our personal best.

DECIDE NOT TO COMPARE YOURSELF WITH OTHERS

For years, I struggled trying to be like my friend, my husband, my pastor's wife, and others. I seemed to find myself constantly comparing myself with someone and in the process rejecting and disapproving of the person God created me to be. After years of misery, I finally understood that God does not make mistakes; He intentionally makes all of us different, and different is not bad. The fact that everyone is different simply showcases God's creativity and the interesting variety He is capable of displaying.

The Bible teaches us that God intricately forms each of us in our mother's womb with His own hand and that He writes all of our days in His book before any of them take shape (Psalm 139:13, 16). As I said, God does not make mistakes, so we should accept ourselves as God's creation and let Him help us be the unique, precious individuals that He intends for us to be.

Confidence begins with self-acceptance, which is made possible through a strong faith in God's love and plan for our lives. I truly believe that we insult God, our Maker, when we compare ourselves with others and desire to be what they are. Let me encourage you to make the decision that you will never again compare yourself with someone else. Appreciate others for who they are and enjoy the wonderful person you are.

I often say that confidence is all about focusing on what you can do and not worrying about what you can't do. Some people work so hard to improve in their areas of weakness that they neglect or overlook their strengths. Confident people do not concentrate on their weaknesses; they maximize their strengths. When we are busy making the most of our strengths, we no longer have time or desire to compare ourselves with others.

QUESTIONS TO HELP YOU GROW IN CONFIDENCE

1. In what areas do you struggle most with comparison? Looks? Possessions? Intellect? Talents and abilities? Accomplishments? Education? Others?

2. Think about your strengths for a moment. List as many of your best qualities as you can think of here. They may not be things you can do, but personality traits such as kindness, discipline, or being a dependable friend.

CONFIDENCE BOOSTERS

Now you [collectively] are Christ's body, and individually [you are] members of it [each with his own special purpose and function].

1 Corinthians 12:27 AMP

We do not dare to classify or compare ourselves with some who commend themselves. When they measure themselves by themselves and compare themselves with themselves, they are not wise.

2 Corinthians 10:12

Pay careful attention to your own work, for then you will get the satisfaction of a job well done, and you won't need to compare yourself to anyone else.

Galatians 6:4 NLT

CHAPTER 6

Just Be Yourself

Be who you were created to be,
and you will set the world on fire.

St. Catherine of Siena

One of the many benefits of confidence is that it empowers us to live authentically. We can be exactly who we are, exactly as God created us to be, in all of our specialness and uniqueness—with no regrets, and no apologies. What a free and happy way to live! When we have confidence, we never feel the need to compare or compete with anyone. Being confident also means we don't have to pretend to be somebody we aren't in order to feel good about ourselves in relation to other people, because we are secure in who we are—even if we're different from those around us.

I believe that confidence gives us permission to be different, to be unique. God has created every person in a unique way, yet many people spend their lives trying to be like someone else—and feeling miserable as a result. Trust me, you can be sure of this: God will never help you be anyone but yourself. He wants you to be you.

NO MORE PRETENDING

The primary reason many people pretend to be someone they are not is that they want to please other people. Wanting to please people is a common desire, and in itself it is not negative or wrong in some ways. But many times people find that they simply cannot be what others want them to be, so they make a big mistake by deciding to pretend so that others will accept them or think highly of them. They try to "fake it 'til they make it."

Faking it, or pretending to be someone you are not, is being untrue to yourself, which is something you should never do. Jesus did not appreciate the hypocrites or the phonies in His day, so you can be sure that He does not want you or me to pretend either. Even if the person you are right now is not who you want to be or know you should be, at least be real. You will grow and change over time, but God loves and accepts you just the way you are right now, so you can love and accept yourself too.

Don't spend your life pretending that you like things you don't like, or frequently being with people you don't enjoy and pretending that you do. To some people, this might sound very "un-Christian," but it really isn't. Jesus told us to love everyone, but He did not say we had to love being with everyone. Some people are more compatible with us than others, and that is okay. There are people that we simply don't fit with—and people we do. Our personalities don't blend or work well together with

everyone else's personalities, and we can grow frustrated
or exhausted pretending to like people who are not a good
match for us. We can ask God to help us behave properly
when we need to be together, but trying to be in a close
working relationship or trying to force a friendship day in
and day out—pretending to enjoy it when we don't—is
not beneficial for anyone.

We should love everyone and be willing to help them
if they have a need. We should not say unkind things
about anyone or critically judge them. We should show
other people respect and realize they are valuable to God.
But we don't necessarily need to spend a lot of time with
people if we don't have shared interests or simply don't
blend well together.

Sadly, the world is full of pretenders. People pretend
to be happy when they are miserable, and they try to do
jobs that are way over their heads because they feel they
should do them in order to be admired or to maintain
a certain reputation. People have many masks and can
become quite adept at changing them as circumstances
require.

I believe that not being true to oneself is one of the
biggest confidence thieves that exists. People can pretend
to be confident, and perhaps others fall for the charade,
but deep inside, pretenders know they are faking it. Ralph
Waldo Emerson pointed out that "To be yourself in a
world that is constantly trying to make you something

else is the greatest accomplishment." Be yourself, and you'll find your confidence.

HAVE FRIENDS WHO GIVE YOU SPACE TO BE YOURSELF

Some people seem to prefer being around us if we pretend or put on a false persona that appeals to them, but there are those rare individuals who actually encourage individuality and value us just the way we are. Spending time with those who accept and affirm us increases our confidence and our enjoyment of life.

One of the many qualities I have appreciated about my husband, Dave, over the years is that he gives me space and even encourages me to be myself. For example, I am a person who likes to spend time alone. When I know I need a few hours or even a few days to have my space, I can simply tell Dave. He is not insecure at all when I need some time alone to study, write, pray, or simply be in a quiet place to think. He does not wonder if something is wrong with me, nor does he feel I am rejecting him. He simply understands that needing time by myself is just the way I am. I am around many people much of the time and am ministering to them, which I love doing. But in order to have balance in my life, I also need to be alone sometimes.

Dave and I work together, we travel together in our ministry, we see each other more than most average married couples, and we enjoy it. But there are times when we need to get away from each other. Dave plays golf, hits golf balls for several hours, or goes to baseball or football games, which gives him the space he needs.

There are evenings when I say to Dave, "Why don't you go out and hit some golf balls? I need an evening alone." He says, "Okay, see you later." A few times each year I try to get away by myself to reflect, read, pray, and just be quiet for several days at a time, and Dave is always understanding of my need. A couple of times each year, Dave takes a several-day golf trip with his golf buddies, and it is good for him to do that.

I am grateful that Dave so graciously accommodates my need to be alone at times. I have met many women whose husbands were offended when their wives had this need or felt personally rejected because of it. The truth is, to nurture healthy relationships, we must give people the space and freedom they need. I'll never forget what one woman said to me: "People energize my husband, and he wants someone around all the time, but people wear me out." I've noticed that there are times when she stays home while he goes somewhere to be with people, and it is fine for them to do that.

Being married to someone who is secure enough to encourage you to be who you are and help you celebrate your uniqueness and individual needs is wonderful. Nobody wants to be made to feel as though something is wrong with them because they want to do something other than what everyone else is doing.

Of course, if we want to be encouraged in our own individuality and independence, we must sow the same type of freedom and respect into other people's lives. We should realize that they have their own needs and desires, and that they may need to pursue certain interests apart from us or spend time alone, as I have needed to do. When we support their expressions of uniqueness, we give them confidence, and we feel confident too. We know our relationships are solid, and we are secure enough to allow others to grow and do what they need to do, just as they allow us to fulfill the needs that we have.

Many relational problems and even divorces are caused by someone trying to make another person what they want them to be instead of accepting them as they are. People will love you if you give them freedom, but they will resent you if you try to manipulate and control them for your own benefit.

ENJOY THE JOURNEY

Occasionally people say they are not sure who they really are. Perhaps they have spent so many years trying to be like someone else that they have lost themselves. If this describes you, let me encourage you to begin now purposefully discovering and expressing who you really are. If you have spent years having to fulfill responsibilities that have not allowed you the freedom to find out who you are and express yourself without reservation, this may take time, but it can be a wonderful adventure. Don't be discouraged if it takes a while; just enjoy the journey. You will find great freedom and joy in being yourself. If you'd like to discover more about who you really are and how to experience the joy of being yourself, I believe you would find my book *Authentically, Uniquely You* very helpful.

QUESTIONS TO HELP YOU
GROW IN CONFIDENCE

1. What is stressful about pretending? How can you avoid
   being trapped by it?

2. Why is being your true, authentic self so important?

CONFIDENCE BOOSTERS

*I praise you because I am fearfully and wonderfully made;
your works are wonderful, I know that full well.*

Psalm 139:14

*Am I now trying to win the approval of human beings, or of
God? Or am I trying to please people? If I were still trying to
please people, I would not be a servant of Christ.*

Galatians 1:10

*The Lord does not look at the things people look at. People look
at the outward appearance, but the Lord looks at the heart.*

1 Samuel 16:7

CHAPTER 7

Stand Up for Yourself

Stand up to your obstacles and do something about them. You will find they haven't half the strength you think they have.

Norman Vincent Peale, *The Power of Positive Thinking*

Becoming your most confident self involves learning to stand up for yourself and developing what I call "balanced independence." This means being able to trust and depend on God and other people in healthy, appropriate ways, yet also establishing your own individual identity—a strong sense of who you are and what you can do for yourself without needing other people's approval. Don't lose the power God has given you to be an individual.

John 15:5 says that we can do nothing apart from God. And Philippians 4:13 says, "I can do all things through Christ who strengthens me" (NKJV). When we consider Philippians 4:13 and John 15:5 together, we see that without Christ, we *are nothing* and we *can do nothing*. But with Him, we are everything He wants us to be, we have everything He intends for us to have, and we can do everything He calls us to do. Because this is true, we can be confident and we can live in balanced independence.

When we recognize our need for God and our total dependence on Him as well as our need for healthy human relationships, we gain the balance we need in order to become independent in appropriate ways. This includes fulfilling our responsibilities and taking care of ourselves physically, financially, emotionally, socially, and spiritually. It also includes being able to stand up for ourselves by having our own opinions, learning to say no and to set appropriate boundaries when necessary, and dealing with criticism. Let's look at each of these individually.

FORM YOUR OWN OPINIONS

Opinions are not truths or facts; they are viewpoints, beliefs, or perspectives. According to the *Merriam-Webster .com Dictionary*, an opinion is "a view, judgment, or appraisal formed in the mind about a particular matter." Simply put, your opinion is what you think about something.

People's opinions vary greatly, and every person has a right to think as they choose. It's important for you to develop your own opinion on certain matters and not allow other people or public opinion to influence you to change it unless you have good reason to do so. Sometimes we change our opinion because we have heard and considered someone else's viewpoint, and it is good to be able to do so. Or, over time, you may change your opinions, but they will hopefully evolve as a result of gaining new insights, perspectives, or information—not because other people pressure you to change your mind.

Confident people know what they believe and why they believe it, and they are comfortable expressing their opinions graciously, kindly, and respectfully. When others disagree with them, they are not intimidated. They do not attempt to change anyone else's mind, but they don't let anyone change their mind either.

You are entitled to your opinion, but that doesn't mean you should always share it. Be wise enough to know when to talk about it and when to keep quiet.

The Bible says that Jesus "knew that the Father had put all things under his power, and that he had come from God and was returning to God," put on a towel and washed the disciples' feet (John 13:3–5). The Amplified Bible, Classic Edition version of this scripture indicates that He put on a "servant's" towel. He was able to do this seemingly lowly task because He knew who He was and had no need to impress anyone. He was truly the greatest among them, and He was the ultimate servant.

SAY NO WHEN NECESSARY

Another way to stand up for yourself is to say no when it is the wise course of action for you. Anyone who says yes to everyone all the time is headed for trouble. When

people want you to do something, they won't be happy if
you tell them no, but sooner or later you must decide if
you will spend your time and energy making other people
happy or if you will pursue happiness for yourself within
God's will.

A confident person can say no when they need to.
They can endure people's displeasure and understand that
if they disappoint someone who truly wants relationship
with them, that person will ultimately want them to be
free to make their own decisions. In healthy relationships,
both parties encourage each other to follow the guidance
of the Holy Spirit and say no when needed, and they support each other in doing so.

Sometimes you have to say no to others in order to
say yes to yourself. Otherwise, you will end up bitter and
resentful, feeling that somewhere in the process of trying
to keep others happy you lost yourself. You may have a
desire to please people, especially close friends or family
members, but it is important to be led by God and stay
balanced in this area. Always remember that you are valuable and that you need to do things you want to do as well
as doing things for others.

If you are like many people, you may have a tendency
to want to explain yourself when you say no to someone.
Perhaps you think they will accept the no better if you
have a good reason for saying it. But there are also times
when you cannot explain why you had to say no. You may

say no because you don't have God's peace about saying yes, and you don't know why. There is a reason, but God may not reveal it until later.

Recently I was asked to do something, and after giving it some thought, I realized that when I thought about doing it, I didn't feel peaceful. I simply told the people making the request that I didn't have peace at that time about saying yes to it. Thankfully, they are mature Christians who said, "We don't want you to do anything you don't have peace about." These are the type of people I consider to be good friends—those who respect my rights and actually want me to follow God more than they want me to follow them.

People often want us to justify our decisions, but we can resist that temptation. We simply need to be led by God's Spirit (another way of saying this is to say we need to follow our hearts) when deciding to say yes or no to requests, opportunities, or commitments. This is what I have learned to do. Sometimes I don't fully understand why I don't feel something isn't right for me, but I have learned that if I do feel that way, I should not go against my own conscience in order to make someone happy. I often say, "I just don't have peace about it," or "I don't feel right about it." Mature people will respect your no, even when you do not know how to explain it.

LEARN TO COPE WITH CRITICISM

The third way you can stand up for yourself is to learn to cope with criticism. Life seems to be full of critics, and no matter what you do, someone may speak negatively about you. Criticism is difficult for most of us to hear, and one critical remark can damage a person's self-image. For this reason, it is important to learn to deal with criticism and not let it bother you.

I encourage you to know yourself, know what's in your heart, have your own opinions, and not let criticism cause you to sway from them. People may judge you, but you can choose not to let their judgment affect you. You may or may not choose to respond to the criticism with words or actions, but you can always handle it in your heart by refusing to believe it while also choosing to forgive the person who criticized you. Always ask God if the one criticizing you is right, because it is important to be teachable and make appropriate adjustments. But don't become offended or angry and give the devil a foothold in your life.

The apostle Paul experienced much criticism. He learned, as we need to learn, that people are fickle. They love you when you do everything they want you to do and are quick to criticize when you do even one little thing they do not like. Paul said that he was not at all concerned about the judgments of others. He said that he did not even judge himself (1 Corinthians 4:3–4). He knew that the only judge who matters is God, and we will all one day stand before Him, not before other people.

Sometimes people who are criticized the most are the ones who work hardest to do something constructive with their lives. I am amazed when people who do nothing want to criticize those who try to do something. I may not always do everything right, but at least I am attempting to do something to make the world a better place and to help hurting people. I believe this is pleasing to God. After many years of suffering because of criticisms and trying to gain people's approval, I finally decided that if God is happy with me, that is enough. I hope that will always be enough for you too.

Learning to stand up for yourself is necessary for becoming a truly confident person. You can do this by living with balanced independence, developing your own opinions and sticking with them unless God leads you to change them, saying no when you need to say no, and learning to deal with criticism. God has made you special and unique. No one has a right to try to change your mind about that or to criticize who He has made you to be or what He has called you to do.

QUESTIONS TO HELP YOU GROW IN CONFIDENCE

1. What do you need to say no to in your life? What do you need to say yes to?

2. What can you do to stay balanced when others criticize you, or when their opinions differ from yours?

CONFIDENCE BOOSTERS

Be on your guard; stand firm in the faith; be courageous; be strong.

1 Corinthians 16:13

Do not judge, or you too will be judged. For in the same way you judge others, you will be judged, and with the measure you use, it will be measured to you.

Matthew 7:1–2

Therefore, there is now no condemnation for those who are in Christ Jesus.

Romans 8:1

CHAPTER 8

Be Positive

Never yield to gloomy anticipation.
Place your hope and confidence in God.
He has no record of failure.

Lettie Cowman

A positive attitude is a necessary and defining quality of a confident person. Confident people think positive thoughts, speak positive words, and have a positive expectation for everything they do. They know that confidence and negativity are like oil and water and simply do not mix.

I was once a very negative woman. But, thank God, I finally learned that being positive is much more fun and fruitful, and it is the will of God. I have chosen to be positive ever since. We all have a choice: We can be negative or we can be positive. This decision determines how we think, speak, and act. We make the choice, and then we become either positive or negative people by building positive or negative habits through repetitious behavior. Looking on the bright side of life is just as easy as looking on the dark side. Why not believe something good will happen instead of presuming things will turn out bad?

If you struggle with negativity, your background may be similar to mine. I grew up in a negative atmosphere around negative people. They were my role models, and I learned to think and act as they did. I did not realize my negative attitude was a problem until I married Dave. He was very positive and began asking me why I was so negative. As I started thinking about it, I realized that I had always been that way. No wonder my life was so negative! I began to understand that I never expected anything good—so I never got it. Being negative led to many problems and disappointments in my life, which further fueled my negativity. It took time for me to change, but I am convinced that if I can change, anyone can.

I truly believe one of the biggest reasons people resist thinking positively is that they have convinced themselves that if they do not expect anything good to happen, they will not be disappointed if it doesn't. This is a sad way to live, and people who think this way are mistaken. This kind of thinking actually causes them to live in disappointment. Every day is filled with disappointment for a person whose thoughts and expectations are negative. But for those who think positively and expect positive outcomes, every day is filled with hope and joy. This does not mean that nothing disappointing ever happens.

Disappointments come along for everyone, but not as often for those who think positively. When disappointments do happen, a positive attitude enables people to deal with them better than a negative one. Keep in mind that if you have lived with a negative attitude and negative circumstances for a long time, it will take time to turn it around. Don't have unrealistic expectations. Things will change, but you need to give your new positive attitude time to turn negative circumstances around.

POSITIVITY IS GOD'S REALITY

Some people say that they resist thinking positively because "that's not reality." But the truth is that positive thinking can change your current reality. God is optimistic all the time; positivity is His reality. It is the way He is, the way He thinks, and the way He encourages us to be. According to Romans 8:28, "In all things God works for the good of those who love him, who have been called according to his purpose."

A common statistic tells us that 90 percent of what we worry about never happens. This makes me wonder why people assume that being negative is more realistic than being positive. We simply need to choose whether we want to look at things from God's perspective or not.

Keep in mind that the devil lies to us and tells us that our circumstances will be bad. He then tempts us to think accordingly, so we must be able to recognize what he is doing and resist it immediately.

Since God is positive and the devil is negative, let me ask you: Who is doing your thinking for you? Have you renewed your mind according to God's Word (Romans 12:2), so you can think as He thinks? Are you choosing your thoughts carefully so they are positive and in agreement with His Word? Or do you allow the enemy to influence your thinking? The enemy wants you to think negatively, but God wants you to think positively. Thinking negatively prevents you from being aggressive, bold, and confident in healthy ways. Why not think positively and live confidently?

STAYING POSITIVE THROUGH SETBACKS

Being positive is easy as long as everything is going well for you. But when circumstances turn negative because you face disappointments or make mistakes, that's when you'll need to make an extra effort to stay positive.

Setbacks are not failures. You are never a failure because you try some things that do not work out. The only way to fail is to stop trying. Instead of allowing mistakes to stop you, let them teach and train you. I say that if I try something and it does not work, at least I know not to do it again.

Many people are confused about what to do with

their lives. They don't know what God's will is for them; they are without direction. I once felt the same way, but I discovered my destiny by trying several things. I tried working in the nursery at church and quickly discovered that was not my calling. I tried being my pastor's secretary, but after one day I was fired with no explanation except "This just isn't right." I was devastated at first, until I was asked to start a weekly women's meeting teaching God's Word at church. I quickly found where I fit. I could have spent my life being confused, but I thank God that I was confident enough to step out and discover what was right for me. I did it through the process of elimination, and I experienced some disappointments, but everything worked out well in the end.

If you are doing nothing with your life because you are not sure what to do, pray and begin trying some different things. God will lead you to something that is a perfect fit for you. Think of it this way: When you go out to buy a new outfit, you may try on several pieces of clothing until you find what fits right, feels comfortable, and looks good on you. Why not use this approach while discovering your destiny? Obviously, there are some things you cannot just "try"—such as being an astronaut or professional dancer—but one thing is for sure: You cannot drive a parked car. Get your life moving in some direction.

I don't suggest going into debt to find out if you

should own a business, but you could begin in some small way and, if it works, take it to the next level. As you take steps of faith, your destiny will unfold. God will make His will clear to you. Look for open doors in your life, because this is one way that God speaks to people. He opens right doors and closes wrong ones. A confident person is not afraid to make mistakes, and if they do, they recover and press on.

God always provides new beginnings. His mercies are new every morning (Lamentations 3:22–23). Jesus chose disciples who had weaknesses and made mistakes, but He worked with them and helped them become all that they could be. He will do the same for you, if you will let Him. Let go of what lies behind you and press toward the things ahead (Philippians 3:13). Be confident and optimistic about the future instead of staying stuck in your past.

Recovering from pain or disappointment is a choice—a decision to let go and move forward. Gather up the fragments of your mistakes and give them to Jesus, and He will make sure that nothing is wasted (John 6:12). Refuse to dwell on what you have lost, and begin looking for opportunities to use what you still have.

Not only can you recover from your setbacks, but God can also use you to help other people recover from theirs. Be a living example of a confident person who always bounces back, no matter how difficult or frequent the setbacks may be. Don't ever say, "I just cannot go on." Instead say, "I can do whatever I need to do through Christ who strengthens me. I will never quit, because God is on my side." Knowing that God is with you and that He is for you will help keep you positive and confident in every situation.

QUESTIONS TO HELP YOU
GROW IN CONFIDENCE

1. In what areas of your life are you tempted to think negatively? How can you change your thinking so you can be positive instead?

2. Think of someone—maybe someone you know or someone you have read about—who has overcome many setbacks with God's help. How does this person inspire you to deal with your challenges?

CONFIDENCE BOOSTERS

I can do all things through Christ who strengthens me.

Philippians 4:13 NKJV

"For I know the plans I have for you," declares the Lord, "plans to prosper you and not to harm you, plans to give you hope and a future."

Jeremiah 29:11

If God is for us, who can be against us?

Romans 8:31

CHAPTER 9

Speak Confidence

There is power in words.
What you say is what you get.

Zig Ziglar

According to Matthew 12:34, whatever is in your heart comes out of your mouth, through your words. And what you say with your mouth affects your heart. Thoughts and words flow in a cycle, and people often wonder which comes first. It really doesn't matter, because they affect each other, and as you learned in the previous chapter, both your thoughts and your words need to be positive in order for you to be most confidently you. In this chapter, I want to focus specifically on the power of words because you can truly change your life with the words you speak.

Consider this amazing truth in Proverbs 18:21: "The tongue has the power of life and death, and those who love it will eat its fruit." According to this verse, the power of life and death is in the words we speak, and we often have to eat them, meaning to be accountable for them. For the tongue to have "the power of life and death" means that our words can be positive, uplifting, encouraging, and helpful in a situation, or they can be negative, discouraging, and detrimental.

I have taught for years about the power of the words we speak, but I believe it bears repeating in this book because it is such an important lesson for us to remember. As long as we are talking, there is power on our lips. Let's use that power to benefit others when we speak to them and to build our confidence when we talk to or about ourselves.

BE CAUTIOUS WITH YOUR WORDS

Until we realize how powerful our words are, we may use them carelessly and pay little attention to what we say. Think about it: How often do you casually say things you would not say if you thought they would actually happen, such as "This situation makes me sick," "I am sick and tired of this," or "This is driving me crazy." I understand that these are figures of speech or common ways of conveying strong feelings in certain situations, and these are a few examples of many. But really, who wants to be sick, or sick and tired, or crazy? I'm sure you see my point. We often say things we don't really mean and would never want to happen.

This brings me to a specific phrase I believe we should be diligent about not using if we want to grow in confidence. People say it often without even realizing what they are speaking. How many times have you said or heard "I'm afraid…" For example:

- "I'm afraid I will never lose weight."
- "My company has been sold, and I'm afraid the new owner will let me go."
- "I'm afraid my kids will get in trouble."
- "I'm afraid it's going to rain."
- "With the way prices are going up, I'm afraid I won't have enough money."
- "I'm afraid if I don't go to that party, people will think badly of me."
- "I'm afraid we won't get a good seat at the theater."
- "I'm afraid we're going to be late to our appointment."
- "I'm afraid the refrigerator is about to go out."

If we heard a recording of every time we have said "I'm afraid," we would probably be amazed that our lives are going as well as they are.

If we really understood the power in our words, I think we would change the way we talk. Our talk should be confident and bold, not fearful. Fearful talk not only affects us in adverse ways, but it can also have a negative impact on the people around us. If you are a parent, for example, and your children frequently hear you say that you are afraid, over time, will that inspire them to be confident, or will it encourage them to be anxious and fearful?

I want to make a bold statement right now: If you will simply change the way you talk and stop casually saying you are afraid, you will begin to feel stronger, bolder, more courageous, and less afraid.

James 3:8 says, "No human being can tame the tongue." I believe this means that we cannot discipline our words without God's help. We are so accustomed to speaking certain words without paying attention to them that we definitely need His help simply to recognize fearful, negative, foolish, silly, and sinful talk.

Even after we recognize the need to be more careful about our speech, we still need to act on that realization and develop new habits in our speech. Forming new habits takes time, so don't get discouraged with yourself if it happens slowly. Keep at it, and little by little, you will develop the habit of saying things that add to your life, not take away from it.

SPEAK LIFE TO YOURSELF

The best way I know to be sure you are speaking life is to speak in agreement with God's Word and to speak it aloud. Don't talk about yourself according to the way you feel, think, or look. Speak what God says over your life; don't say about yourself what others say unless what they say agrees with what He says.

Perhaps your parents, teachers, or friends spoke to you in a way that caused you to lack confidence. They may not have intended to harm you, but their words had a negative impact. I want you to know that those words do not have to influence you anymore. You can declare that those old words are not true and that they have no power over you. You can also change the words you speak about yourself, which will change your image of yourself.

Even if you have had a longtime habit of speaking negatively about yourself, you can change, starting today. Resist the urge to make comments such as "I just don't have any confidence," or "I'll never overcome my fears." Anything God says you can have, you can have, as long as you are in agreement with Him. Here are some examples:

1. The psalmist said that his confidence is in the Lord (Psalm 71:5), so you can declare that your confidence is also in Him.
2. Philippians 4:13 says, "I can do all things through Christ who strengthens me" (NKJV), so you can say, "I can do whatever God tells me to do in life because Christ will give me strength."
3. 2 Timothy 1:7 says, "For God has not given us a spirit of fear, but of power and of love and of a sound mind" (NKJV), so you can say, "I will not fear; God has not given me a spirit of fear. He has given me power, love, and a sound mind."

I'm sure you get the idea, and now you can find many scriptures to speak aloud and apply to your life. To get started, you might consider using the ones at the end of each chapter of this book.

As you speak God's Word aloud, you renew your mind, meaning that you can change the way you think and feel about yourself (Romans 12:2). Stop saying, "I'm depressed and discouraged," "I'm ready to give up," or "Nothing good ever happens to me." This kind of talk is self-defeating. Words such as these cannot add to your life, but they can certainly prevent you from enjoying it.

If you have considered yourself a person with low self-esteem and low confidence, one who is shy and fearful, I believe today can be a turning point for you. However, you will have to be persistent. Speak God's Word again and again. Let it renew your mind more and more. God's Word always has power in it, and when you believe it and speak it consistently, it will change your life.

When you speak confidently, it influences the people around you. When you sound confident in yourself, they will be confident in you also. Don't be arrogant, but do be confident. Start talking and walking with confidence, and expect wonderful things to happen in your life.

QUESTIONS TO HELP YOU
GROW IN CONFIDENCE

1. Ask God to help you pay attention to your words and notice how many times you say the word *afraid* (or any other negative word). What can you do to change your speech to be more positive and confident?

2. What are several examples of life-giving words you will begin to speak over yourself? Say those words every time you are tempted to speak negative words.

CONFIDENCE BOOSTERS

Set a guard over my mouth, Lord; keep watch over the door of my lips.

Psalm 141:3

The one who has knowledge uses words with restraint, and whoever has understanding is even-tempered.

Proverbs 17:27

Words from the mouth of the wise are gracious, but fools are consumed by their own lips.

Ecclesiastes 10:12

CHAPTER 10

Confident People Take Action

A humble man is not afraid of failure.
In fact, he is not afraid of anything....
Thomas Merton, *New Seeds of Contemplation*

Confident people are people of action. They do not sit around and wait for good things to happen; they prayerfully move forward, doing what they know to do and trusting God to guide them to their next steps. Some people, though, hesitate to move forward for various reasons, and their lives come to a standstill. They become stagnant. When this happens, they do not enjoy their lives, they don't do anything to benefit others, and they do not fulfill the purposes for which they were created. Everyone can have a slow day once in a while, but when a confident person sees that their life has reached the point of stagnation, they shake it off and get moving in a positive direction.

When a puddle of water is stagnant, the water does not circulate, and fresh water has no way to get into it.

The water simply sits. Over time, if the sun doesn't evaporate it first, bacteria can thrive and the water can turn green. The water can actually become unhealthy.

People can become stagnant too. Stagnation can happen to anyone at any time, and it happens a little bit at a time and often so slowly that it is almost imperceptible. When we stop experiencing and expressing joy, when we no longer want to take risks, when our dreams and visions for our life grow dim, when life seems boring and we feel predictable, when our creativity wanes, or when we feel we have so many problems that we can't do anything productive—these are good signs stagnation has set in. Stagnation is an enemy of confidence, because where stagnation is, lethargy, despair, discouragement, and even depression can follow.

Stagnation takes place for many reasons—stress, laziness, becoming too busy, increased responsibilities, or simply losing interest in activities that were once exciting and fun. One of the major causes of stagnation is fear. People often refuse to move forward because they are afraid they will make a mistake, afraid they will fail, afraid others will ridicule or reject them, afraid their friends and families won't understand and support them. Or they may be afraid they will be out of God's will, or perhaps they are afraid of all the unknowns that lie ahead of them if they take a confident step of faith. They are so afraid of the negative possibilities involved in moving forward that they do not even consider the positive potential of stepping out and trying something. Confidence is the opposite of fear, and that's why confident people do all they can do to avoid stagnation.

HOW TO STAND AGAINST STAGNATION

I believe everyone will stagnate if they don't actively resist it. It is easy to just float along with everyone else doing the same thing every day. Only rare individuals are willing to swim upstream when drifting downstream with everyone else would be so easy. One of the most valuable lessons I have learned in my life is that there are many things I must do "on purpose." I can't wait to feel like doing them, and sometimes my flesh does not want to do them, but I do them anyway. This is one way I stand against stagnation and keep my confidence level high.

For example, I deliberately take care of my responsibilities, because I know it is very important. I also give to others on purpose. I actually look for people I can bless because I have learned the importance and joy of generosity. I intentionally do something a bit out of the ordinary for me every once in a while, simply because I refuse to live in stagnation. I also intentionally spend time every day in prayer and fellowship with God because I want to honor Him and always give Him His rightful place in my life, which is first place. In addition, I do practical things that keep me from becoming stagnant. As a simple, practical way of keeping variety in my life, I wear different pajamas almost every night. Some people could wear the same nightclothes and never get tired of doing it, but it would bore me.

Whatever it takes for you to keep your life interesting, do it on purpose. If you do this intentionally, it will make a big difference in your quality of life. Don't just put in your time here on earth; instead enjoy your life and make the world glad that you are here. You can't do that if you sit around like a puddle, so resist stagnation and keep your life fresh, vibrant, and confident.

GOD CREATED YOU TO BE PRODUCTIVE

Many times, people feel stagnant and they want to do something, but they don't do what they long to do because they are afraid. Some people are actually so afraid to do something that they form a habit of doing nothing. They sit idly by and become jealous of the people who have the life they would like to have. They become resentful because things never work out for them. They fail to realize that things cannot work out for them if they don't at least make an effort to do something productive.

I know a man who has allowed himself to become very passive due to some painful and disappointing circumstances in his life. I recently asked him if he had taken care of a certain thing that is one of his responsibilities, and he answered, "I just don't have any motivation to do it." He is allowing his feelings to control his decisions instead of doing what he knows he should do, and the longer he allows this passive attitude to rule his life, the more difficulty he will have getting rid of it.

Productivity is good for all of us. As a matter of fact, God said we should work six days and rest one (Exodus 31:15). That's what He did when He created the world (Genesis 2:2), and it shows how important work and activity are in His eyes. God has created us to work, to enjoy the life He has given us, and to make a difference in the world, not to sit idly by doing nothing.

If you feel your confidence is a bit low right now, may I suggest that you just do something? Find a way to get up and get going in a direction that makes you happy and helps you feel you are contributing to the world around you. There are several good stories in the Bible about people who were not doing anything due to illness or infirmity. In a number of those situations, they asked Jesus for help, and He simply told them to "get up"!

One well-known Bible story of someone who needed to get up is the story of the man at the pool of Bethesda. He was an invalid, and he knew that if he could be the first person into the pool when the water was stirred, he would be healed, but he lay there year after year, waiting for someone to help him into the pool.

Then one day, Jesus went to the pool and saw this man lying on his mat, as usual, and learned that he had been there for thirty-eight years. He asked the man a very important question: "Do you want to get well?" (John 5:6).

The man answered: "I have no one to help me into the pool when the water is stirred. While I am trying to get in, someone else goes down ahead of me" (John 5:7).

Jesus responded immediately: "Get up! Pick up your mat and walk" (John 5:8). The man was cured instantly, and he started walking.

For thirty-eight years, that man had felt sorry for himself, so he just lay there and did nothing. The answer to his problem surfaced when he made an effort to move. You may think you are waiting on God, but maybe He is waiting for you to simply "move."

A lack of confidence will keep you still and stagnant, lying on your mat, so to speak. But an attitude of faith and a willingness to get up and do something productive will cause you to feel confident again. And the more confident you are, the more productive, the more fulfilled, and the happier you will be. I believe that if we do what we can do, God will do what we cannot do.

QUESTIONS TO HELP YOU GROW IN CONFIDENCE

1. In what area of your life do you feel stagnant? What can you do on purpose to move forward from that place?

2. Is there something you would really like to do, but you are afraid to move forward with it? What small step can you take to break stagnation and begin to overcome fear?

CONFIDENCE BOOSTERS

Never be lacking in zeal, but keep your spiritual fervor, serving the Lord.

Romans 12:11

Whatever your hand finds to do, do it with all your might.

Ecclesiastes 9:10

So I commend the enjoyment of life, because there is nothing better for a person under the sun than to eat and drink and be glad. Then joy will accompany them in their toil all the days of the life God has given them under the sun.

Ecclesiastes 8:15

CHAPTER 11

Overcoming Fear, the Enemy of Confidence

If the Lord be with us, we have no cause of fear.
His eye is upon us, His arm over us,
His ear open to our prayer—His grace sufficient,
His promise unchangeable.

John Newton, *Cardiphonia*

Some people have a high level of confidence, and some have very low confidence. High confidence empowers people to live boldly and without fear, while low confidence is characterized by timidity, fear, and anxiousness. High confidence serves people well, while low confidence keeps them from enjoying life to the fullest and may hinder them from fulfilling God's plan for their lives. Confidence—the belief that we can succeed—gets us started and helps us finish every challenge we tackle in life. Without confidence, we will live in fear and never feel fulfilled.

People with low confidence are not sure about

anything. They are not only afraid, but they are also indecisive and hesitant, which makes them feel frustrated. When they do make decisions, they are tormented by self-doubt. They second-guess (and third- and fourth-guess) themselves. As a result, they don't live boldly. They have small, narrow lives, and they miss out on the big, rewarding lives God wants them to enjoy.

If you are a person with low confidence, don't worry, because you can change and become a bold, confident person. As you take even tiny steps of faith, God will help you. Each time you succeed and realize that God can be trusted, it will build more confidence for your next faith adventure.

Low confidence is caused by a lack or deficiency of one quality (confidence) and too much of another (fear). Fear is the number one enemy of confidence, and it is not from God. It begins as a thought in your head and then affects your emotions and behaviors. It is a dangerous condition, because a fearful person has no confidence and therefore cannot reach their potential in life. They won't step out of their comfort zone to do anything—especially something new or different. They may truly want to do certain things or make certain changes in their life, but fear makes them unable to do so. Therefore, they end up conflicted and frustrated.

It breaks my heart when I see people living fearfully and without confidence, because without confidence, they can never know and experience true joy and fulfillment. I also believe the Holy Spirit Himself is grieved when we lack confidence, because He has been sent into our lives to help us fulfill our God-ordained destinies. But you can't discover and fulfill your destiny when you've let fear of failure, fear of rejection, fear of people, or other fears control your life.

When we have confidence, we can reach truly amazing heights. We feel there is nothing we cannot do without God's help, so we boldly go after what we hope to experience or achieve. But without confidence, we can lose our ability to hope for more than we currently know. Even simple accomplishments are beyond our grasp. This is not the way God wants us to live. Throughout the Bible, He calls us to live in faith, which is simply confidence in Him.

I HAD TO DO IT AFRAID

I still remember the fear I felt when God called me to quit my job and prepare for ministry. At times, my knees shook and my legs felt so weak that I wasn't sure I could stand. Had I let fear stop me all those years ago, where would I be today? What would I be doing? Would I be happy and fulfilled? Would I be writing a book on being a confident person—or would I be sitting at home, depressed and wondering why my life had been such a disappointment? I believe the reason many people are unhappy and unfulfilled is that they let fear rule their lives.

What about you? Are you doing what you believe you should be doing at this stage in your life? Or have you allowed fear and lack of confidence to prevent you from stepping out into new things—or stepping up to higher levels of old things? If you don't like your answer to those questions, I have good news for you: It is never too late to begin again! Don't spend one more day living a narrow life that only has room for you and your fears. Decide right now that you will learn to live boldly, aggressively, and confidently. Don't let fear rule you any longer.

You can't just sit around and wait for fear to go away. You will have to feel the fear and take action anyway. Courage is not the absence of fear; it is action in the presence of fear. Bold people do what they know they should do, not what they feel like doing. That's what I had to do, and you may need to do it too. Confidence is not the absence of fear, but taking action in the presence of fear.

YOU CAN FEEL FEAR
AND CHOOSE CONFIDENCE

When David went to fight Goliath, he did not stand for hours looking at the enormous giant, wondering how to win the battle against him. The Bible says that David "ran quickly toward the battle line," all the time talking about the greatness of God and declaring his victory ahead of time (1 Samuel 17:48). David did not run away from

his giant; he courageously ran toward him. Neither did
he stand and stare at the giant for a long period of time,
thinking of all the terrible things the giant might do to
him. He followed his heart and didn't give his head time
to talk him out of it.

Do you ever feel certain you should do something,
but you think about it for such a long time that you talk
yourself out of it? I know I have. But we can learn to be
led by God's Spirit, not by our misguided ideas that are
fueled by fear.

Had David run from Goliath, he would never have
been king of Israel. God had anointed him to be king
twenty years before he wore the crown (1 Samuel 16:13).
During those years, he faced his giants and proved that
he had the tenacity to endure difficulty without quitting.
Those experiences helped qualify him to later become
king.

Did David feel any fear as he approached Goliath?
I think he did. Many of his writings are included in the
Bible, and in them, he never claimed to be free from fear.
In fact, he wrote about being afraid, saying: "When I
am afraid, I put my trust in you. In God, whose word I
praise—in God I trust and am not afraid. What can mere
mortals do to me?" (Psalm 56:3–4).

David was clearly saying that even though he *felt* fear,
he chose to *be* confident. You may feel afraid at times too,

but you, like David, can choose to be confident in God. Being confident in the presence of fear requires us to step out and trust that God will be there to help us. And the good news is that if you are wrong and it becomes clear that you have made a mistake, you can simply step back and try something else. The question *What if I am wrong?* stops many people from living confident lives, but as the old saying goes, it's better to have tried and failed than never to have tried at all.

EMBRACE ALL GOD HAS FOR YOU

I believe this book may offer the encouragement you need to take important steps in the direction of your destiny—the life God intends for you to live and enjoy. That life has been waiting for you since the beginning of time. If you have been missing it because of fear or intimidation, then it's time to face every fear, overcome every obstacle, and finally embrace everything God has for you.

Satan is the master of intimidation, and once you realize he is the one behind your fear or hesitation, you can take authority over him by simply resisting him, placing your confidence in Jesus Christ, and stepping out boldly to be all you can be. God said to Joshua, "Do not be afraid; do not be discouraged, for the Lord your God will be with you wherever you go" (Joshua 1:9). He is speaking that same message to you today. Fear not! God is with you, and He will "never leave you nor forsake you" (Deuteronomy 31:6).

Abraham was told that "God is with you in everything you do" (Genesis 21:22). That sounds like large living to me. Are you ready for a larger life, one that leaves you feeling satisfied and fulfilled? I believe you are, and I want to do everything I can do to help you on your journey.

QUESTIONS TO HELP YOU
GROW IN CONFIDENCE

1. Where in your life has fear held you back? How would your life change if you trusted God to give you courage to face the fear and become confident in that area?

2. Think about an area in which you *feel* afraid. What would it look like for you to *choose* confidence?

CONFIDENCE BOOSTERS

The wicked flee though no one pursues, but the righteous are as bold as a lion.

Proverbs 28:1

Do not fear, for I have redeemed you; I have summoned you by name; you are mine.

Isaiah 43:1

When I am afraid, I put my trust in you.

Psalm 56:3

CHAPTER 12

Confidence Can Help You Manage Stress

Oh, how great peace and quietness would he possess who should cut off all vain anxiety... and place all his confidence in God.

Thomas à Kempis, *The Imitation of Christ*

Stress is a big problem in most people's lives today, perhaps yours. Everything is so fast paced, loud, and excessive that our mental, emotional, and physical systems stay on overload. We are inundated with information via websites, social media, and twenty-four-hour news. We're on information overload, and it is no wonder we have trouble calming our minds down so we can rest. In addition to the vast amounts of information the world throws at us each day, we have schedules that seem busier than ever. We often feel unable to find enough hours in any day to do what we need to do, much less what we want to do. In addition, we sometimes feel we need to do certain things in order to be accepted in certain social circles or to be promoted at work. We hurry and rush; we feel pressured, frustrated, and tired; and it's not uncommon for us to think, *I'm under so much stress that I feel I'm about to explode!*

In addition, if we are parents, we want our children to be like all the other children, so we let them get involved in far too many activities, most of which require some involvement from us also. Sometimes, having children who participate in too many activities puts families under financial stress. The children want the same clothing, shoes, and equipment that others have. If you have ever bought your child a two-hundred-dollar pair of tennis shoes that you could not afford just because "everyone has them," then you know exactly what I mean.

Also, if we experienced rejection as children, we can understandably be afraid our sons and daughters will be also rejected, and we want to spare them that painful experience. This helps make the point I want you to understand in this chapter: While we think our stress comes from being busy, much of it actually comes from some type of fear.

THE REAL ROOT OF MUCH STRESS

You read in the previous chapter that fear is the enemy of confidence, and in this chapter, you will see how fear is also the root of many of our stresses. Think about it: We often become involved in things simply because we are afraid of missing out or being left out. We are often afraid we won't know what is going on or that someone else will gain control of a situation if we are not there to be involved personally or to speak for ourselves. We may also be afraid others might criticize us or look down on us if we say we don't want to be involved in certain activities.

There are times when we become so afraid of displeasing other people that we say yes to activities or commitments when we know we should be saying no to them. When this happens, our stress comes from being afraid of rejection or disapproval, not from having too much to do.

Often, we wear ourselves out because we are afraid to be different, so we desperately try to keep up with all the other people in our lives. We may force ourselves to attend a social event when we know we are too tired to go and, truthfully, would much rather order takeout and watch a movie at home. We go to the event anyway because we don't want people to think we are boring or don't want the hosts to think we don't like them. When we keep pushing ourselves to do things we don't want to do, we end up stressed.

HOW TO DO MORE WITH LESS STRESS

Part of being a confident person means being sure that whatever you are involved in is something you definitely need to be doing. Doing things out of desire affects us very differently than doing them out of fear or other unhealthy motives. God will not energize our fears, but

He does energize us if we have faith that we are doing the right things and approach our projects and activities with confidence in Him.

Fear drains you of whatever energy you might have and leaves you feeling stressed to the max, while confidence and faith actually energize you. Confident people can do more with less stress because they live with an ease and a grace that fearful people never experience.

As you can see, I don't believe that *what* we do creates stress nearly as much as *how* we do it. If we do something fearfully and under pressure with no real desire to do it, then stress and misery result. If you have been under a lot of stress lately, I encourage you to take an honest inventory of not only what you are doing but why you are doing it. If fear is the reason you're involved in something, then eliminate some stress by getting your priorities straight. Your priority is not to keep everyone else in your life happy by doing what they expect; it is to live a life that is pleasing to God and that you can enjoy.

Too many people are not living their dreams because they are living their fears. In other words, instead of doing things from their heart, they do them because they are afraid of what will happen if they don't. They think, *Someone will be angry. I will get left out! People will talk about me!* The truth is, most people are so focused on themselves that they don't think as much about anyone else as much we sometimes assume they do.

Let me encourage you to evaluate the reasons you are doing what you currently do. If you are doing anything because of fear, then eliminate it. Ask God to lead you concerning the way you spend your time. You will be amazed at how much time you may have if you have a Spirit-led schedule rather than a people-driven one.

It is time that you started being the person you really want to be. It is time to reach for your dreams. What has God placed in your heart? Is there something you want to do that you have been waiting on? I believe God's timing is very important, and I certainly don't think we should take action foolishly, but some people spend their entire life "waiting on God," and sometimes God is waiting for them to take action.

Feeling frustrated and unfulfilled creates stress. Nothing is more stressful than going through the motions of life every day and still feeling at the end of each week, month, or year that you are no closer than you ever were to reaching your dream or goal. Let me encourage you today to be confident in the dreams and desires God has put in your heart. Instead of doing things because you are afraid of what people will think if you don't do them, pour your energy into thoughts and activities that will help your God-given goals become realities by His grace.

QUESTIONS TO HELP YOU GROW IN CONFIDENCE

1. How does fear cause stress in your life? How does that stress affect you?

2. Make a list of tasks that stress you. Then write down enjoyable activities or commitments that are fulfilling to you. Ask God to help you prioritize these for a confident and more stress-free life.

CONFIDENCE BOOSTERS

Do not be anxious about anything, but in every situation, by prayer and petition, with thanksgiving, present your requests to God. And the peace of God, which transcends all understanding, will guard your hearts and your minds in Christ Jesus.

Philippians 4:6–7

Let the peace of Christ rule in your hearts, since as members of one body you were called to peace. And be thankful.

Colossians 3:15

You will keep in perfect peace those whose minds are steadfast, because they trust in you.

Isaiah 26:3

CHAPTER 13

Confidently Reach Out to Others

Those who are happiest are those who do the most for others.

Booker T. Washington, *Up from Slavery*

People who live with confidence in God trust Him to meet their every need and to take care of everything that concerns them (Psalm 138:8 NKJV). They are not overly focused on their own provision or well-being. They believe the promise of Philippians 4:19 for themselves and want God to use them to help others experience it too: "And my God will meet all your needs according to the riches of his glory in Christ Jesus." Therefore, they are happy to help or bless others when they see a chance to do so, in whatever way—big or small—may be needed. They know they can help people close to them in the simplest way by smiling and being friendly or by holding a door open when someone has their hands full. They also know that they can benefit people who live on the other side of the world by donating to missions or charities that work in underprivileged nations. They train themselves to look for needs of any kind, and they are quick to do whatever they can do to help others.

People without confidence usually won't offer to help others because they fear being rejected. I recall wanting to pay for someone's coffee at a coffee shop one day, and the person simply refused to let me do so. It was a bit embarrassing because other people saw what was going on, but I am not going to let an incident like that prevent me from reaching out to other people. A less confident person might allow a situation such as that one make them fearful of trying again. It is our responsibility to do what we believe God is guiding us to do, no matter how other people respond.

Some individuals pass quietly through life, not making the impact they could make because they lack the confidence they need to make a difference in the world or to bless others. They spend their time and energy taking care of their needs and making sure they are provided for. They don't think much about doing something—even seemingly small—to make the world a better place. The fact is, though, that nothing they do is insignificant if it helps make someone's life easier or their burden lighter.

While it is responsible to be wise stewards of our resources and to provide for ourselves and our families, the Bible also instructs us to help others and to be generous (Proverbs 22:9). Philippians 2:4 addresses this specifically, saying: "Let each of you look not only to his own interests, but also to the interests of others" (ESV). We have opportunities each day to help people, if we will simply be aware of them and step up to do whatever we can do to assist.

Just think about it: Someone at your job may be caring for elderly family members and could use some extra help meeting a deadline. Someone in your life may be disappointed, and a smile or an encouraging word from you would lift their spirits. Someone you know may have lost a spouse recently, and they would love a phone call or a visit because they are lonely. Perhaps a neighbor has just been diagnosed with a debilitating disease, and a casserole, a bowl of fresh fruit, or a plate of muffins would be comforting. Or maybe a family at church is in danger of losing their home because one spouse lost their job and hasn't been able to find another one for months. The bank is ready to foreclose on their loan, and they really have nowhere else to go. They are desperate and don't know what to do. Everyone tells them that God will provide, but no one is doing anything. Could you offer them a place to live or ask several other people to pitch in with you to meet this family's expenses for a month or two?

Many times, when we think of helping people, we think of obvious needs, such as the ones I have just mentioned. One place we sometimes forget to look when we think of people we can help is right under your own roof.

Perhaps your spouse or one of your children could use some affirmation or words of appreciation. Maybe a child is struggling in school and needs your undivided attention to help with their homework. You may not have to go very far to help or bless someone in a big way.

God is always eager to help and provide for people, but He works through other people—perhaps you. We are His hands, feet, arms, mouth, eyes, and ears. God does miracles, but He often does them through people with the awareness to recognize the needs around them and the confidence to say, "I would love to help you!"

YOU CAN BE AN ADD-ER
OR A SUBTRACT-ER

When God created Adam and Eve, He blessed them and told them to be fruitful and multiply and use all the vast resources He gave to serve Himself and others (Genesis 1:28). So let me ask you: Are you being fruitful? When you get involved with people, do situations get better, not worse? Some people only take in life, and they never add anything. They don't even put a smile on someone else's face. I refuse to be that kind of person. I want to make people's lives better, and I'm sure you do too. It's a blessed way to live.

Jesus told the story of a man who had so much that all of his barns were full, with no room to hold any more. Instead of giving any of it away, he decided to tear down the barns he had and just build bigger ones to collect more stuff for himself (Luke 12:16–18).

He could have chosen to use what he had to bless others, but he must have been a fearful, selfish man, who only had room in his life for himself (Luke 12:19). God called the man a fool and said, "This very night your life will be demanded from you. Then who will get what you have prepared for yourself?" (Luke 12:20). The man would die that night, and all he would leave behind were his material possessions. He had an opportunity to make the world a better place. He could have added to many lives and put smiles on thousands of faces. Instead, he fearfully and selfishly cared only about himself.

Jesus said that if we want to be His disciples, we will lose sight of our personal interests and focus on serving Him (Mark 8:34). The minute we hear that, we tend to think, *What about me? If I forget myself, who will take care of me?* Believe me when I say that God Himself will take care of you. Everything you do for other people will come back to you and bring you joy, many times over. If you are willing to give yourself away, you will enjoy a much better life than you would ever experience if you stay overly focused on trying to take care of yourself.

I hope you will refuse to selfishly and fearfully pass through this life and do everything you can, in every way you can, for everyone that you can, as often as you can. If that is your goal, you will be one who makes the world a better place and puts a smile on people's faces.

Be courageous when you see someone in need, and start doing all you can to help others. Have confidence that God will meet all your needs, and begin to ask Him to give you the resources to meet the needs of people around you. Ask Him to make you a generous person who is eager to bless others. As you help and bless them, their confidence in God will increase and they will see that they can trust Him to do what they need Him to do in their lives. The more confident they become, the more they will reach out to other people; as a result, multitudes will soon be blessed simply because others had confidence in God to meet needs and were not afraid to help or provide for those around them.

QUESTIONS TO HELP YOU GROW IN CONFIDENCE

1. What can you expect to happen when you are generous, according to Luke 6:38?

2. Who can you bless this week? How?

CONFIDENCE BOOSTERS

Give, and it will be given to you. A good measure, pressed down, shaken together and running over, will be poured into your lap. For with the measure you use, it will be measured to you.

Luke 6:38

What good is it, my brothers and sisters, if someone claims to have faith but has no deeds? Can such faith save them? Suppose a brother or a sister is without clothes and daily food. If one of you says to them, "Go in peace; keep warm and well fed," but does nothing about their physical needs, what good is it? In the same way, faith by itself, if it is not accompanied by action, is dead.

James 2:14–17

If anyone has material possessions and sees a brother or sister in need but has no pity on them, how can the love of God be in that person?

1 John 3:17

CHAPTER 14

Perseverance Builds Confidence

Faith is a living, daring confidence in God's grace,
so sure and certain that a believer would
stake his life on it a thousand times.

Martin Luther, "Preface to the Epistle to the Romans"

All of us are running a race, so to speak, in life, and we should run to win. A confident person believes they will win but knows that winning requires preparation, training, sacrifice, and a will to persevere—to press past opposition. This may require failing many times but then getting up, starting again, and continuing despite any opposition they may encounter. Discouragement and fear quit when the going gets tough, but confidence and courage finish.

As you go through life, you will find that what is best for you in certain situations will not always be what is easy. Sometimes doing your best or getting the best result requires extra effort. Opposition is common when you are trying to do something God has called you to do, so don't let it surprise you. As you seek to overcome it, you may be tempted at times to do what is easy instead of what is best. If you will stand against that temptation, defeat the opposition against you, and keep going, you will reach your goal. When you face situations or obstacles that threaten to wear you down, be confident that you *will* succeed if you simply keep moving forward.

Winning in life doesn't mean that we engage in fierce competition against others so we will always take first place, but that we dig down deep into ourselves, do our very best, and persevere to finish what we start. Are you tempted to give up on something right now? Don't! I urge you to press on, because overcoming your challenge and finishing your race will allow you to trust yourself—and God—more, and that is very important in building your confidence.

YOU CAN EXPECT OPPOSITION

In the beginning of my ministry, God gave me a dream one night while I was sleeping. In it, I was driving down the highway, and I noticed cars pulling off to the side of the road. Some were parking, and others were turning around to go back where they came from. I assumed there must be trouble ahead, but I could not see what it was. As I boldly continued to drive forward, I saw a bridge with water from the river below starting to flow across it. I realized that the people in the cars were afraid they might get hurt trying to cross the bridge, or that they would reach their destination and then not be able to get back. The dream ended with me sitting in my car looking first at the water-covered bridge, then back to where I had been, and then at the side of the road, trying to decide whether to park, retreat, or keep moving forward.

God used that dream to show me that opposition presents itself when we are pressing toward a goal. There will always be opportunities to park and go no farther or to turn around and give up. In the dream, I had to decide each time if I would give up or go on. That dream has helped me many times to press on when difficulties came and I was tempted to quit.

I have decided that even though I don't always do everything right, and I may not always get the result I hope for, I will never quit. Determination and perseverance will get you a lot further than talent. So if you feel you lack in talent, take heart. All you need to win in life is plenty of perseverance and a determination to never quit. As long as you keep going, you will eventually gain victory.

CONFIDENT PEOPLE NEVER QUIT

As a confident person, quitting simply is not an option for you. You must decide what you want or need to do and make up your mind to finish your course. You will experience some opposition no matter what you attempt to do in life. The apostle Paul said that when doors of opportunity opened to him, opposition came with it (1 Corinthians 16:9). Confidence believes that, with God, it can handle whatever comes its way; it doesn't fear what has not happened yet.

When you attempt to do something and fear rears its ugly head, you must remember that *the goal of fear is to stop you.* Fear wants you to run, withdraw, and hide. Fear is of the enemy, and the enemy wants you to give up and then be upset with yourself for quitting. God wants you to finish what you start.

The apostle Paul had a God-given assignment, and he was determined to complete it, even though he could suffer and even be imprisoned (Acts 20:22–23). He kept his eyes on the finish line, not on what he knew he would go through. He said he wasn't moved by the opposition, but that his goal was to finish his race "with joy" (Acts 20:24 NKJV). Paul not only wanted to finish what he started; he wanted to enjoy the journey.

When we are confident in God, we can enjoy what He calls us to do. But enjoyment is not possible if we are afraid all the time. Fear brings present torment concerning future situations that may not happen anyway. Paul knew that whatever did happen, God would be faithful to strengthen him so that he might patiently endure it without quitting.

KEEP YOUR EYES ON THE PRIZE

You always have a choice about where you put your focus. You can focus on the positive or on the negative. You can fix your gaze on God and all that He can do, or you can lock your attention onto the enemy and all the ways he tries to defeat you and stop God's plan for your life. Let me encourage you to keep your eyes on the prize—the goal to which God has called you—not on the pain or opposition you encounter as you pursue it.

The apostle Paul was no stranger to opposition and difficulty, but his confidence was in Christ, just as ours is. His perspective on the hardships he faced is a good example for all of us: "We are hard pressed on every side, but not crushed; perplexed, but not in despair; persecuted, but not abandoned; struck down, but not destroyed" (2 Corinthians 4:8–9). In spite of this opposition, he went on to say:

> *Therefore we do not lose heart. Though outwardly we are wasting away, yet inwardly we are being renewed day by day. For our light and momentary troubles are achieving for us an eternal glory that far outweighs them all.* So we fix our eyes not on what is seen, but on what is unseen, since what is seen is temporary, but what is unseen is eternal.
>
> 2 Corinthians 4:16–18, emphasis mine

My heart is stirred with courage as I read these words of Paul, and I hope your heart is stirred too. He made up his mind that no matter what happened, *he would finish his course*. He did face opposition, but he did not grow discouraged, because he looked not at the things he could see but to what he could not see. He kept his eyes on God. Some people will encourage you, but others may try to discourage you, so decide ahead of time not to believe what people say more than you believe what God has said to you.

If we think and talk about our problems too much, they are likely to defeat us. I like to say, "Glance at your problems, but stare at Jesus." We don't deny the existence of problems, and we don't ignore them, but we do not permit them to rule us. We think about God and His power more than we think about the obstacles we face. Any problem we have is subject to change, especially as we persevere through it: "With God all things are possible" (Matthew 19:26).

QUESTIONS TO HELP YOU GROW IN CONFIDENCE

1. When you face opposition, what does fear want you to do? What does confidence in God encourage you to do instead?

2. Think about a problem you have now, and apply this advice to it: "Glance at your problems, but stare at Jesus." List practical ways you can focus on Jesus as you deal with this problem and run your race.

CONFIDENCE BOOSTERS

Therefore, since we are surrounded by such a great cloud of witnesses, let us throw off everything that hinders and the sin that so easily entangles. And let us run with perseverance the race marked out for us, fixing our eyes on Jesus, the pioneer and perfecter of faith. For the joy set before him he endured the cross, scorning its shame, and sat down at the right hand of the throne of God.

Hebrews 12:1–2

Not that I have already obtained all this, or have already arrived at my goal, but I press on to take hold of that for which Christ Jesus took hold of me.

Philippians 3:12

Brothers and sisters, I do not consider myself yet to have taken hold of it. But one thing I do: Forgetting what is behind and straining toward what is ahead, I press on toward the goal to win the prize for which God has called me heavenward in Christ Jesus.

Philippians 3:13–14

CONCLUSION

In this book, I have shared much that I know about how to become confidently you. I believe you will act on this information and begin living boldly and fearlessly. I hope one lesson you have learned through this book is that it doesn't matter what kind of personality you have, you can choose to be confident. Confidence may come more easily to some personality types than to others, but confidence is a decision, and you can choose today that you *will* be confident. It may or may not produce a feeling, but don't ever let your feelings cast the deciding vote when you are making decisions.

I hope you realize as a result of this book that the past is behind you and that your past does not determine your present or your future. This is a new beginning. Every day, God's mercies are new, and they are available for all of us today (Lamentations 3:22–23). Don't look back; look ahead!

As you move into the great future God has for you, know that a confident appearance will help you feel more confident and inspire the people around you to be confident in you too. So put a big smile on your face, make eye contact with people, stand up straight, hold your shoulders back and your head high, and walk like you have somewhere to go. You are full of life, and you are beloved of God, so act like it!

Let me close this book with a few reminders: Be decisive, follow your heart, don't let fear cause you to shrink back from anything you want to do or anything to which God calls you, and don't be overly concerned about what other people think of you and your decisions. Don't live constantly comparing yourself with others; be your unique self (2 Corinthians 10:12). Celebrate who God has made you to be. There is only one person on all the earth who has the unique traits and skills that make up who you are. Enjoy the fact that God knew what He was doing when He created you, and He has made you to fulfill a special purpose, to enjoy your life, and to bless others as long as you live.

Finally, I hope you will remember to live your life with a confident expectation of the Lord, trusting Him in every situation. Ephesians 3:20 tells us that God is able to do exceedingly and abundantly above and beyond all that we could never dare to hope, ask, or think. Are you daring in prayer? Are you expecting enough? The devil wants us to believe we must go to God with head hung low, telling Him how terrible we are. He wants us to believe that we dare not ask for too much, because after all, we don't deserve anything.

Satan is afraid of bold, daring, confident, fearless, and

expectant prayer. Start praying like you have never prayed before. Pray expectantly, boldly, fearlessly, and confidently. Believe that God wants to meet your needs because He is good, not necessarily because you are good. None of us living in a fleshly body has a perfect record; we all make mistakes, and yours probably are no worse than anyone else's. So stop beating up on yourself and start expecting God to be God in your life.

Be confident even when you don't *feel* confident, and watch God do amazing things in your life. I am cheering you on!

SCRIPTURE NOTATIONS

Unless otherwise noted, Scripture quotations are taken from the Holy Bible, New International Version®, NIV®. Copyright ©1973, 1978, 1984, 2011 by Biblica, Inc.™ Used by permission of Zondervan. All rights reserved worldwide. www.zondervan.com The "NIV" and "New International Version" are trademarks registered in the United States Patent and Trademark Office by Biblica, Inc.™

Scripture quotations marked NLT are taken from the Holy Bible, New Living Translation, copyright ©1996, 2004, 2007, 2013, 2015 by Tyndale House Foundation. Used by permission of Tyndale House Publishers, Inc., Carol Stream, Illinois 60188. All rights reserved.

Scripture quotations marked AMP are from the Amplified® Bible Copyright © 2015 by The Lockman Foundation Used by permission. www.lockman.org

Scripture quotations marked ESV are taken from The Holy Bible, English Standard Version. ESV® Text Edition: 2016. Copyright © 2001 by Crossway Bibles, a publishing ministry of Good News Publishers.

Scripture quotations marked NKJV are taken from the New King James Version®. Copyright © 1982 by Thomas Nelson. Used by permission. All rights reserved.

Scripture quotations marked AMPC are taken from the Amplified® Bible, Copyright © 1954, 1958, 1962, 1964, 1965, 1987 by The Lockman Foundation Used by permission. www.Lockman.org.

Do you have a real relationship with Jesus?

God loves you! He created you to be a special, unique, one-of-a-kind individual, and He has a specific purpose and plan for your life. And through a personal relationship with your Creator—God—you can discover a way of life that will truly satisfy your soul.

No matter who you are, what you've done, or where you are in your life right now, God's love and grace are greater than your sin—your mistakes. Jesus willingly gave His life so you can receive forgiveness from God and have new life in Him. He's just waiting for you to invite Him to be your Savior and Lord.

If you are ready to commit your life to Jesus and follow Him, all you have to do is ask Him to forgive your sins and give you a fresh start in the life you are meant to live. Begin by praying this prayer . . .

Lord Jesus, thank You for giving Your life
for me and forgiving me of my sins so I can have
a personal relationship with You. I am sincerely
sorry for the mistakes I've made, and I know
I need You to help me live right.

Your Word says in Romans 10:9, "If you declare
with your mouth, 'Jesus is Lord,' and believe in
your heart that God raised him from the dead,
you will be saved" (NIV). I believe You are the Son
of God and confess You as my Savior and Lord.
Take me just as I am, and work in my heart,
making me the person You want me to be.
I want to live for You, Jesus, and I am so grateful
that You are giving me a fresh start in my
new life with You today.
I love You, Jesus!

It's so amazing to know that God loves us so much! He wants to have a deep, intimate relationship with us that grows every day as we spend time with Him in prayer and Bible study. And we want to encourage you in your new life in Christ.

Please visit joycemeyer.org/salvation to request Joyce's book *A New Way of Living*, which is our gift to you. We also have other free resources online to help you make progress in pursuing everything God has for you.

Congratulations on your fresh start in your life in Christ! We hope to hear from you soon.

ABOUT THE AUTHOR

Joyce Meyer is one of the world's leading practical Bible teachers. A *New York Times* bestselling author, Joyce's books have helped millions of people find hope and restoration through Jesus Christ. Joyce's programs, *Enjoying Everyday Life* and *Everyday Answers with Joyce Meyer*, air around the world on television, radio, and the internet. Through Joyce Meyer Ministries, Joyce teaches internationally on a number of topics with a particular focus on how the Word of God applies to our everyday lives. Her candid communication style allows her to share openly and practically about her experiences so others can apply what she has learned to their lives.

Joyce has authored more than 130 books, which have been translated into more than 100 languages, and over 65 million of her books have been distributed worldwide. Bestsellers include *Power Thoughts*; *The Confident Woman*; *Look Great, Feel Great*; *Starting Your Day Right*; *Ending Your Day Right*; *Approval Addiction*; *How to Hear from God*; *Beauty for Ashes*; and *Battlefield of the Mind*.

Joyce's passion to help hurting people is foundational to the vision of Hand of Hope, the missions arm of Joyce Meyer Ministries. Hand of Hope provides worldwide humanitarian outreaches such as feeding programs, medical care, orphanages, disaster response, human trafficking intervention and rehabilitation, and much more—always sharing the love and Gospel of Christ.

JOYCE MEYER MINISTRIES
U.S. & FOREIGN OFFICE ADDRESSES

Joyce Meyer Ministries
P.O. Box 655
Fenton, MO 63026
USA
(636) 349-0303

**Joyce Meyer Ministries—
Canada**
P.O. Box 7700
Vancouver, BC V6B 4E2
Canada
(800) 868-1002

**Joyce Meyer Ministries—
Australia**
Locked Bag 77
Mansfield Delivery Centre
Queensland 4122
Australia
(07) 3349 1200

**Joyce Meyer Ministries—
England**
P.O. Box 1549
Windsor SL4 1GT
United Kingdom
01753 831102

**Joyce Meyer Ministries—
South Africa**
P.O. Box 5
Cape Town 8000
South Africa
(27) 21-701-1056

**Joyce Meyer Ministries—
Francophonie**
29 avenue Maurice Chevalier
77330 Ozoir la Ferriere
France

**Joyce Meyer Ministries—
Germany**
Postfach 761001
22060 Hamburg
Germany
+49 (0)40 / 88 88 4 11 11

**Joyce Meyer Ministries—
Netherlands**
Lorenzlaan 14
7002 HB Doetinchem
+31 657 555 9789

**Joyce Meyer Ministries—
Russia**
P.O. Box 789
Moscow 101000
Russia
+7 (495) 727-14-68

OTHER BOOKS BY JOYCE MEYER

BOOKS BY DAVE MEYER